OBJECTIVE

IELTS

Michael Black
Annette Capel

Workbook with Answers

Advanced

CAMBRIDGE
UNIVERSITY PRESS

CAMBRIDGE UNIVERSITY PRESS
Cambridge, New York, Melbourne, Madrid, Cape Town, Singapore, São Paulo

Cambridge University Press
The Edinburgh Building, Cambridge CB2 2RU, UK

www.cambridge.org
Information on this title: www.cambridge.org/9780521608787

First published 2006
Reprinted 2006

Printed in the United Kingdom at the University Press, Cambridge

A catalogue record for this book is available from the British Library

ISBN 13 978-0-521-60878-7 Workbook with Answers
ISBN 10 0-521-60878-3 Workbook with Answers

ISBN 13 978-0-521-60879-4 Workbook
ISBN 10 0-521-60879-1 Workbook

ISBN 13 978-0-521-60884-8 Student's Book
ISBN 10 0-521-60884-8 Student's Book

ISBN 13 978-0-521-60883-1 Self-study Student's Book
ISBN 10 0-521-60883-X Self-study Student's Book

ISBN 13 978-0-521-60875-6 Teacher's Book
ISBN 10 0-521-60875-9 Teacher's Book

ISBN 13 978-0-521-60876-3 Cassette Set
ISBN 10 0-521-60876-7 Cassette Set

ISBN 13 978-0-521-60877-0 Audio CD Set
ISBN 10 0-521-60877-5 Audio CD Set

Designed and produced by Kamae Design, Oxford

Contents

Information overload

Reading

1 Read this passage quickly to get a general idea of its meaning. Don't worry if you don't understand every word. Time yourself as you read.

⏱ about 350 words

Reading as part of writing

1

One of the techniques of writing successfully in an academic environment is to be able to integrate the important points of what you have read into your own writing. To do this, you must have a clear picture of what you have read, and this in itself entails active and focused reading. With academic reading, it is necessary to maintain a constant grip on what the author is saying. Yet many academic texts are densely written in unfamiliar ways, which make them much more difficult to manage than, for example, a novel or a magazine article.

2

Although sometimes there may be reasons why you need to skim-read an article or book, this is likely to be only to get the gist of what is being said, as a way of deciding whether it is appropriate reading material or not. In general, skim-reading is not a particularly useful strategy for a student, but you may well be used to doing this in other contexts, for example, skimming through a newspaper article or surfing the web. Instead of skim-reading, you will be developing ways of concentrating on large chunks of quite dense text and making sense of them.

3

Even though you may only be reading for short bursts of time, it is likely that you will have to concentrate far more intensely on academic reading material than, for example, when reading for pleasure. You don't necessarily have to work in the library, but you will need to decide what type of location and atmosphere suits you best, and establish conditions that are conducive to effective study.

4

The initial stumbling block that most students face is choosing their reading. The first thing to do is to consult the reading list you have been given for books and articles that seem relevant to your particular assignment. Doing a library search, by key words or subject, is also useful if the references on your reading list are already on loan from the library. Your tutor should also be able to advise you as to which are the most relevant publications or websites.

2 Decide on a suitable heading (A–E) for each paragraph. There is one heading you will not need.

A Selecting your sources
B Creating the optimum environment
C Taking on the scholastic challenge
D Approaching your first essay
E Choosing the most suitable reading skill

3 Find words or phrases in the text that mean the same as these.

1 involves (paragraph 1)
2 keep hold of (paragraph 1)
3 the general meaning (paragraph 2)
4 on different occasions (paragraph 2)
5 extensive extracts (paragraph 2)
6 decoding (paragraph 2)
7 is right for you (paragraph 3)
8 advantageous (paragraph 3)
9 hurdle (paragraph 4)
10 borrowed (paragraph 4)

Vocabulary

4 Find ten more words in the wordsearch to do with visiting a library. The words go horizontally and vertically (→↓).

S	W	A	G	L	E	Y	M	I	Z
P	E	R	I	O	D	I	C	A	L
I	N	E	O	A	R	B	O	S	T
N	E	S	F	N	D	J	S	R	O
E	L	E	C	T	R	O	N	I	C
B	U	L	S	E	A	R	C	H	O
A	S	H	E	L	F	C	A	R	D
I	S	S	U	E	V	O	T	L	E
N	R	E	S	O	U	R	C	E	S
J	O	U	R	N	A	L	A	V	O

5 Use the words from exercise 4 to complete this text for library users.

Welcome to the college library! Use our
1 .... tools to locate
the publications you need. The three-digit
2 .... tells you which part of the library
to go to. For books, you will then have to look for
the catalogue number, which is displayed on the
book's 3 .... If you need to order a
4 .... or 5 .... , you must
fill in a form, stating the 6 .... month
and year. Should a book you need already be out
on 7 .... , you can put in a request
for it. Simply enter your library 8 ....
PIN on screen. Please note that our staffing
9 .... are limited. You can help
by returning all books to the correct
10 .... when you have finished with
them.

Grammar G ··⊹ STUDENT'S BOOK page 138

Modality

6 Choose the correct verb in these sentences.

1 You *needn't / mustn't* leave books on the library tables.
2 Students applying for grants *should / might* submit their forms no later than Friday 20 July.
3 I *haven't / needn't* any alternative but to give you a formal warning.
4 Sam *must / had to* go to a tutorial yesterday afternoon.
5 It *might / can* be possible to have your paper printed in this journal.
6 The university admissions office *ought to / needs to* see the originals of all your certificates by Friday.
7 I *shouldn't / couldn't* find anything useful on the website you recommended.
8 It *may / should* be necessary to cancel Dr Jefferson's ten o'clock lecture.

7 Complete the sentences with a suitable modal perfect.

EXAMPLE: Sally ......*can't have*...... felt well yesterday because she didn't attend class.

1 It looked like Dr Roberts, but it .... been him because he's away at a conference.
2 My essay got such a low mark that the only possible explanation is that I .... misunderstood the question completely.
3 There .... been a bug in the original software, but the new version I've downloaded seems fine.
4 Candidates in the listening test .... been affected by the noise of building work, but it's impossible to be certain of this.
5 You .... been very careful in checking your essay – it's full of spelling mistakes!
6 The poor results from your experiment suggest that you .... measured the amounts properly.

Only a game

Reading

1 Read this extract from an article that appeared in the journal *Scientific American* in July 2004, just before the Athens Olympic Games. Time yourself as you read.

⏱ about 300 words

GENE DOPING

Athletes will be going to Athens next month to take part in a tradition begun in Greece more than 2,000 years ago. As the world's finest specimens of fitness test the extreme limits of human
5 strength, speed and agility, <u>some of them will probably also engage in a more recent, less inspiring Olympic tradition: using performance-enhancing substances</u>. Despite repeated scandals, doping has become irresistible to many athletes, if only to keep
10 pace with competitors who are doing it. Where victory is paramount, athletes will seize any opportunity to gain an extra few split seconds of speed or a small boost of endurance.

Sports authorities fear that a new form of doping
15 will be undetectable and thus much less preventable. Treatments that regenerate muscle, increase its strength and protect it from degradation will soon be entering human clinical trials for muscle-wasting disorders. Among these are therapies that give
20 patients a synthetic gene, which can last for years, producing high amounts of naturally occurring muscle-building chemicals.

This kind of gene therapy could transform the lives of the elderly and people with muscular dystrophy.

Unfortunately, it is also a dream come true for an 25 athlete bent on doping. The chemicals are indistinguishable from their natural counterparts and are only generated locally in the muscle tissue. Nothing enters the bloodstream, so officials will have nothing to detect in a blood or urine test. 30

Is gene therapy going to form the basis of high-tech cheating in athletics? It is certainly possible. Will there be a time when gene therapy becomes so commonplace for disease that manipulating genes to enhance performance will become universally 35 accepted? Perhaps. Either way, the world may be about to watch one of its final Olympic Games without genetically enhanced athletes.

2 Find paraphrases in the text for the statements below. Underline the relevant part of the text. The statements follow the order of information in the text.

EXAMPLE: A few athletes are likely to take drugs to improve their ability.

1 Athletes often feel they have to take drugs in order to match their peers.
2 Athletes are happy to do whatever it takes because winning is all that matters.
3 Those in charge of sport believe that it will be far harder to stop athletes from trying gene therapy.
4 Gene therapy is about to be tested on people whose muscles are very weak.
5 Gene therapy is a very fortunate development for athletes wishing to cheat.
6 The man-made substances are identical to those that exist in the body.
7 Athletes at the Athens Olympics may be among the last generation to compete without gene therapy.

Vocabulary

3 Scan the text to find words that match the definitions below to complete the word puzzle. Which word from the text is revealed vertically?

1 artificial (paragraph 2)
2 equivalents (paragraph 3)
3 undoubtedly (paragraph 4)
4 discover (paragraph 3)
5 impossible to refuse (paragraph 1)
6 remedies (paragraph 2)
7 the process of becoming weaker (paragraph 2)
8 tampering with (paragraph 4)
9 shocking events (paragraph 1)

Grammar (G)···✦ STUDENT'S BOOK page 138

Perfect tenses

4 Put the verbs in the following sentences into a suitable simple or continuous perfect tense.

EXAMPLE: Thompson (not/make) ...*hadn't made*... the first team all season, but last Wednesday he was finally selected.

1 The football club (struggle) .... to stay in the upper half of the table this year.
2 How long (David/play) .... tennis this morning?
3 The company (sign) .... an agreement to broadcast all live ice-hockey matches during next season.
4 (you/set) .... the video to record the highlights while we're out?
5 We (try) .... to organise a diving competition, but it's proving very difficult to fix a date.
6 Harry (not/expect) .... to reach the play-off, so he was thrilled by the result.
7 (the college/enter) .... a team in the volleyball championship?
8 Lance Armstrong (win) .... the Tour de France more than once.

5 Correct any errors in perfect tenses in these sentences written by IELTS candidates, which are taken from the *Cambridge Learner Corpus*. One sentence is correct.

1 As the information age had arrived, people's work and lives have becoming more and more dependent on computers.
2 It happened for the past two weeks, at the same time every evening.
3 I used my lighter to light the candle, but unfortunately I've also lit a book I just read!
4 We have been waiting for 20 minutes before someone came to give us a menu.
5 The computer is one of those inventions that had changed the way we live.
6 Technology has been advancing rapidly at the expense of our traditional skills.
7 There were recent cases in other sports events in which people have injured themselves because of unsafe equipment.

6 Report these sports soundbites, using the past perfect tense.

EXAMPLE: 'Arsenal have beaten Crystal Palace 4–1.'

They announced that ...*Arsenal had beaten Crystal Palace 4–1*... .

1 'Ian Thorp broke the world record for the 50m freestyle earlier today.'
They said that ....
2 'Rusedski has been cleared of drug-taking and the charges against him dropped.'
They announced that ....
3 'Builders have almost completed work on the new stadium.'
They said that ....

3 Brands

Reading

1 **Quickly read this article about changing the image of a Czech car manufacturer. Time yourself as you read.**

⏱ about 425 words

Rebranding Skoda

Back in the 1980s, when I bought my first car, I could only afford a Skoda. It caused great amusement among my friends, who delighted in telling me the jokes going around, jokes like 'Why does a Skoda have a heated rear
5 windscreen? Answer: To keep your hands warm when you push it.' Although I put a brave face on it, <u>I had to agree:</u> Skoda owners couldn't claim to be leaders of fashion. I would never have predicted that, by the end of the century, Skoda would be one of Britain's fastest-growing car brands.
10   The company's change in fortunes began when the Czech government, Skoda's owner, decided the business needed foreign investment. In 1991, it went into partnership with the German car manufacturer Volkswagen, which took full control of Skoda ten years later.

Volkswagen invested over £2 billion in the business, 15 and the first model to be launched by the 'new' Skoda was the Felicia, in 1994. Although motoring journalists were generally positive about it, UK sales were poor.

The Felicia was followed four years later by the Octavia, but only 6,000 cars were sold in its first year, 20 despite good reviews. One reason was that the company's costs were greater now than before, so it could no longer afford to be a cheap brand: it had to convince consumers that Skoda cars gave value for money. In addition, the company still had an out- 25 dated image that no longer matched its products, and market research found that 60% of people claimed they 'would never buy a Skoda'.

The Skoda brand must have seemed a liability to Volkswagen, as the UK is a large car market. However, 30 the cars sold well in Eastern Europe and were moderately successful in most Western European countries. In the UK, Skoda at least had the advantage of high 'brand awareness' – that is, many people recognised the name, even if they remembered it for 35 the wrong reasons.

March 2000 saw the launch of the Fabia, with an advertising message that gently made fun of British consumers' perceptions: 'The Fabia is a car so good that you won't believe it's a Skoda'. The car was an 40 instant success. There was also a shift in the image of Skoda cars in Britain, with the 60% who would not consider buying one falling to 42%. Skoda has successfully been rebranded: now, for many UK customers, a Skoda is a cut-price Volkswagen, and a 45 purchase well worth considering.

And me? Well, I'm again an owner of a Skoda, but this time I'm proud to be one.

2 **Do the following statements reflect the claims of the writer in the passage?** ⋯⟩ TF2

Write

YES   *if the statement reflects the claims of the writer*
NO   *if the statement contradicts the claims of the writer*
NOT GIVEN   *if it is impossible to say what the writer thinks about this*

EXAMPLE: There was good reason for the jokes made about Skoda cars in the 1980s. *YES*
                (See underlined text.)

1 In the 1980s, Skodas were the least popular cars in Britain.
2 The Czech government negotiated with several foreign companies before deciding to work with Volkswagen.
3 Sales of the Felicia were lower than they deserved to be.
4 The Octavia seemed out-dated.
5 Very few British people had heard of Skoda in the 1990s.
6 The Fabia was a better car than the Felicia and Octavia.
7 Many British customers believe Skoda and Volkswagen cars are of a similar quality.

Grammar G ⟶ STUDENT'S BOOK page 139

Cleft sentences

3 Complete the sentences below using phrases from the box. Make sure that each sentence is both grammatically correct and true according to the passage.

> a partnership with another manufacturer
> at the end of the century
> high 'brand awareness'
> in 1994
> in its first year
> in the 1980s
> that the business needed foreign investment
> the Fabia
> the fact that the company's costs had increased
> the Felicia
> the Octavia

1 It was .... that was an instant success.
2 It was .... that I bought my first car.
3 It was .... that Skoda became one of Britain's fastest-growing car brands.
4 It was .... that was launched in 1994.
5 What the Czech government decided was ....
6 What led to a rise in Skoda prices was ....
7 What Skoda benefited from in the UK in the 1990s was ....

4 Complete each sentence with the correct ending from the box.

> A that they are memorable.
> B that companies carry out market research.
> C that we bring meaning into our lives.
> D that Hear'Say was created.
> E that there may be very little difference between rival products.
> F that companies can maximise their sales.
> G that they were a manufactured group.

1 It was through a television contest …
2 What made many journalists interested in Hear'Say was …
3 Some people believe it is by buying products …
4 It is by paying careful attention to marketing …
5 It is to identify consumers' perceptions of their products …
6 What makes some logos effective is …

Vocabulary

5 Complete these sentences using words from Unit 3 of the Student's Book or the passage on page 8. The first letter of each word is given.

1 A l _ _ _ _ is used as a visual reminder of a brand or company.
2 C _ _ _ _ _ _ _ _ _ _ between manufacturers of similar products can keep prices down.
3 Cars and clothing are examples of manufactured g _ _ _ _ .
4 The l _ _ _ _ _ of a product onto the market is when it is introduced and made available for the first time.
5 A person who buys items to meet their own needs is a c _ _ _ _ _ _ _ .
6 M _ _ _ _ _ _ _ is an activity concerned with encouraging people to buy a company's products.
7 The word 'p _ _ _ _ _ _ _' can mean 'to buy', 'the act of buying' or 'something bought'.
8 People's opinion or mental picture of something, for example of a brand, is its i _ _ _ _ .
9 Unlike car manufacturers, banks and training companies sell a s _ _ _ _ _ _ .
10 Shops, market stalls and kiosks are all examples of r _ _ _ _ _ outlets.

4 Spotlight on communication

Vocabulary

1 These words occur in the Vocabulary section of 4.1 of the Student's Book (page 27). Complete each sentence with one word or phrase from the box. You may need to make the word plural.

He was as sick as a parrot.

| accent | acronym | collocation | false friend | idiom |
| jargon | nonverbal communication | proverb | slang |

1 Some .... are pronounced as words, e.g. *radar*, while others consist of letters that are pronounced separately, such as *DJ*.

2 .... which is deliberate, such as smiling and waving, is usually easy to interpret, but when it is involuntary, there is a danger of misinterpreting it.

3 *Nick* (= prison) and *a screw* (= prison warder) are .... expressions that originated in British prisons.

4 The .... *sour grapes* comes from one of Æsop's fables, written about 2,500 years ago.

5 One of the challenges of a foreign language is learning .... , for example, that *traffic* is usually described in English as *heavy*, and not as *strong* or *big*.

6 People who have not studied law generally have difficulty understanding legal .... , with words like a *tort* meaning *harm done to another person or their property*.

Grammar (G) ···⟶ STUDENT'S BOOK page 139

Adverbial clauses

2 Put each of these introductory words and phrases into the right column. Then use a dictionary to check how to use them – ones in the same column don't necessarily have the same meaning.

after	although	as (×2)	as soon as	because	before	even if (×2)
even though	if	once since (×2)	so that	though	unless	until
when	whenever	where	whereas	wherever	while (×2)

Time	Place	Reason	Purpose	Condition	Concession
•	•	•	•	•	• ....
•	•	•		•	• ....
•		•		•	• ....
•					• ....
•					• ....
•					• ....
•					
•					
•					
•					

3 In the reading passage below, <u>underline</u> the adverbial clauses and write their functions in the margin. Remember that clauses must contain a verb. They are used in this order.

1 time	**3** time	**5** reason	**7** reason
2 time	**4** condition	**6** condition	**8** condition

Reading

4 This passage, which comes from a non-specialist book about the English language, is about clichés – words and phrases that are overused. Read it quickly, concentrating on understanding the points that the writer is making: it isn't necessary to understand all the clichés that he uses. Remember to time yourself as you read.

⏱ about 600 words

Clichés

A cliché is a phrase that has been used so many times that it comes out of the mouth or the computer without causing a ripple in the mind of the speaker, the typist, the listener or the reader. **(A)**
5 **The word was part of the technical jargon of the French printing trade in the 19th century, the name for a plate used in the printing process,** and it is still used with that meaning in English and other languages. By the middle of the same century, the word was being
10 used in French, shortly followed by English, as a metaphor for frequently used expressions.

(B) Clichés can be classified according to whether they were originally idioms, similes and proverbs, expressions from trades or invented phrases.

15 Many idioms have been so indiscriminately overused that they have been weakened – phrases like *far and wide*, *by leaps and bounds* or *safe and sound*. Our second category could be similes and proverbs that now fall off the lips with little
20 meaning, **(C) similes like** *as cool as a cucumber* – **which dates back around 400 years –** *as fit as a fiddle*, **and the proverb** *don't put the cart before the horse*.

A large category is drawn from the jargons of trades and professions, sports and games, and other
25 national concerns. **(D) Many are nautical clichés, as is fitting for the British, as an island nation, with examples like** *to leave a sinking ship, to know the ropes, to stick to one's guns.*

Our last broad category of clichés might be
30 phrases which were striking when they were first coined, but have become ineffective through constant use. **(E) When a football manager, asked how**

he felt about the defeat of his team, said that he was *as sick as a parrot*, a reference to the sensational cases of psittacosis from West Africa in the early 35 1970s, it was a sharp, amusing phrase. Since then, it has been so overused that it has lost its shine. *To explore every avenue* and *to leave no stone unturned* are two political clichés of this class. No politician with any sensitivity for language could use 40 either of those phrases seriously, yet you hear them at it still, all the time.

(F) No doubt we could elaborate the classes of clichés into further subdivisions until the cows come home. But there is no need to. We all agree that 45 clichés are to be avoided by careful writers and speakers at all times, do we not? Well, actually, no, not I. Life, and language, are so full of clichés that silence will reign supreme if you deny us the use of cliché. **(G) So many millions of people have spoken** 50 **and written so ceaselessly that it is almost impossible to find ideas and phrases that have not been used many times before.**

Poets and philosophers mint brand new language. The rest of us have to make do with the 55 common currency. It is often the case that clichés become popular because they are the best way of saying something. *Castles in Spain* and *a white elephant* vividly express ideas that would otherwise require far more words. **(H) You would be cutting off** 60 **your nose to spite your face if you denied yourself the use of the brightest, most economical and most beautiful phrases invented, simply because they were clichés.** In short, I am determined to have my cake and eat it, to have my finger in every pie, and to 65 reserve my right to pull a cliché out of the vast cupboard of the English language, if it is the best way of saying what I want to say.

5 The information on the right is found in the parts of the passage printed in bold. Which part (A–H) contains the following information? Consider all eight parts before choosing your answer. Note: In the Reading Modules, the relevant parts of the passage are *not* in bold. ⋯⋗ TF4

1 a claim concerning the difficulty of avoiding clichés
2 examples of clichés originally used in a particular occupation
3 a way of distinguishing between types of clichés
4 a suggestion that clichés should sometimes be used
5 an account of the origin of a particular cliché
6 the original meaning of the word *cliché*

5 Is plastic fantastic?

Reading

1 Read this article that appeared in *New Scientist*. Time yourself as you read.

⏱ about 500 words

WRAPPERS SMARTEN UP TO PROTECT FOOD

Active packaging will tell you instantly if your groceries are fresh.

Unwrapping your shopping to find you have bought mouldy bread, rotten fruit and sour milk could soon become a thing of the past, thanks to a range of emerging 'active packaging' technologies. While
5 conventional packaging simply acts as a barrier that protects food, active packaging can do a lot more. Some materials interact with the product to improve it in some way, or provide better information on the state it is in. For instance, they may soak up oxygen
10 inside a wrapper to help prevent food spoilage or show whether potentially dangerous foods like red meat and chicken have been stored at unsafe temperatures.

One of the new breed of packaging technologies that has just gone on the market in France is a 'time
15 temperature indicator'. Stores where the product has already been introduced report that far fewer consumers are returning spoilt food. The indicator is basically a label that tracks the temperature a package has been kept at and for how long. The label has a
20 dark ring around a lighter circle. The central ring contains a chemical which polymerises, changing colour as it does so from clear to dark. If the package stays cool, the reaction is slow, but increasing the ambient temperature speeds up the polymerisation. When the inner circle darkens, it means the product is no longer
25 guaranteed fresh.

Other indicators are being developed to monitor the gases being given off inside frozen-food packages, causing deterioration – perhaps because of a freezer breakdown. The National Center for Toxicological
30 Research in Arkansas, USA, has developed a plastic disc impregnated with a dye that sits inside food packaging and changes colour if gases produced by decay are present.

Smart packaging can also control the atmosphere
35 inside a container. For instance, the make-up of oxygen (O_2) and carbon dioxide (CO_2) within packaged vegetables will influence their freshness. This can be hard to control in a sealed package, since vegetables consume more oxygen and give off more carbon
40 dioxide as the package gets warmer. A firm in California is trying to solve the problem with a membrane wrapper it calls 'Intelimer', which changes its permeability as the temperature changes in a way that keeps different products at their optimal O_2/CO_2
45 concentrations.

Decay can also be decelerated by controlling the environment inside a package with an 'oxygen scavenger'. Currently, this is achieved by placing a sachet filled with iron powder in the package – any
50 oxygen in the package is consumed by the iron as it oxidises. However, consumers don't like finding sachets marked 'Don't eat' in their food, so a company in New Jersey is making a wrap that itself scavenges oxygen. The material includes an inner layer of an oxidisable
55 polymer that traps oxygen in the same way as iron.

It is predicted that between 20 and 40 per cent of all food packaging will soon be active.

2 Complete the sentences with one or two words from the passage. Remember to check your spelling. ⋯⟩ TF4

1 Active packaging offers far more benefits than
.... kinds, which
merely cover food up.

2 New wrapping materials are being developed to
.... whatever they are
covering, for the benefit of the consumer.

3 A recently developed device that alerts consumers
to a product's storage profile is triggered by the
rate of a chemical ....

4 In the event of mechanical failure in
storage, one new product that is
.... a colorant can
reveal whether food is rotten.

5 The key to keeping packaged vegetables at their
best lies in .... of
oxygen and carbon dioxide.

6 One innovative type of wrapping has an
.... which absorbs
oxygen.

Vocabulary

3 Scan the text to find verbs that collocate with the
nouns and adjective below. Use them to complete
the word puzzle. Write all the verbs in their
infinitive form. Which verb from the text's title is
revealed vertically?

1 spoilage (paragraph 1)
2 temperature (paragraph 2)
3 a product (paragraph 2)
4 cool (paragraph 2)
5 deterioration (paragraph 3)
6 oxygen (paragraph 4)
7 the environment (paragraph 5)

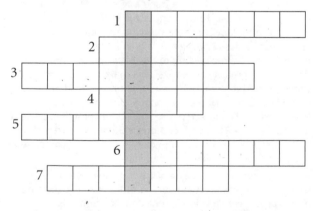

Grammar ⓖ ⋯⟩ STUDENT'S BOOK page 140

Passives

4 Complete the sentences with a verb from the box,
writing it in the passive form given in brackets.

| ~~be~~ | find | ~~invent~~ | keep | ~~make~~ | relate |
| ~~use~~ | | | | | |

EXAMPLE: Food storage (*modal perfect passive*)
must have been very different before the
invention of plastics.

1 This product (*modal present passive*)
.... fresh for at least two weeks
if sealed in plastic and stored in the fridge.

2 Nowadays, many clothes (*present simple passive*)
.... from a blend of cotton and
polyester, which is a form of plastic.

3 The story of plastic dates back to 1870, when a
material known as celluloid (*past simple passive*)
....

4 A German study found that 400% more material
by weight would need (*passive infinitive*)
.... if plastic did not exist.

5 No correlation (*present perfect passive*)
.... between vinyl
manufacturing and cancer.

6 Up to three million full-time jobs in the USA
(*present simple passive*) .... in
some way to the plastics industry.

5 Finish the second sentences so that they mean the
same as the first, using passive forms. The agent
with *by* is not always needed.

EXAMPLE: Active packaging keeps food fresh for
longer.
Food *is kept fresh for longer by active
packaging.*

1 They are producing more goods in plastic.
More goods ....
2 Our local council has just introduced a plastics
recycling scheme.
A plastics recycling scheme ....
3 They use plastics in the manufacture of pills.
Plastics ....
4 They are about to launch a new type of
biodegradable plastic bottle.
A new type of biodegradable plastic bottle ....
5 The factory might shut down its glassmaking
division, to concentrate on plastic.
The factory's glassmaking division ....
6 If someone hadn't invented plastic, what
materials would we be using today?
If plastic ....

6 Music matters

Reading

1 Read this article about downloading music from the Internet by the musician Janis Ian, which comes from her website www.janisian.com. Note the informal style, which is appropriate for the Internet. Time yourself as you read.

⏱ about 825 words

THE INTERNET DEBACLE – AN ALTERNATIVE VIEW

When I research an article, I normally send 30 or so emails to friends and acquaintances asking for opinions and anecdotes. I usually receive between 10 and 20 in reply. This time, I sent 36 emails requesting opinions and
5 facts on free music downloading from the Net. I stated that I planned to adopt the viewpoint of devil's advocate: free Internet downloads are good for the music industry and its artists. I've received, to date, over 300 replies, every single one from someone 'in the music business'.

10 What's more interesting than the emails are the phone calls. I don't know anyone at NARAS (home of the Grammy Awards), and I know Hilary Rosen (head of the Recording Industry Association of America, or RIAA) only vaguely. Yet within 24 hours of sending my original
15 email, I'd received two messages from Rosen and four from NARAS requesting that I call to 'discuss the article'.

The NARAS people told me downloads were 'destroying sales', 'ruining the music industry' and 'costing *you* money'. Costing *me* money? I don't think so. Ms Rosen
20 stressed that she was only interested in presenting the RIAA's side of the issue, and was kind enough to send me a fair amount of statistics and documentation, including a number of focus-group studies the RIAA had run on the matter. However, the problem with focus
25 groups is the same problem anthropologists have when studying peoples in the field – the moment the anthropologist's presence is known, everything changes. Hundreds of scientific studies have shown that any experimental group *wants to please the examiner*. For
30 focus groups, this is particularly true.

The premise of all this nonsense is that the industry (and its artists) are being harmed by free downloading. I don't agree. My site (www.janisian.com) gets an average of 75,000 hits a year. Not bad for someone whose last hit
35 record was in 1975. I've found that every time we make a few songs available on my website, sales of all the CDs go up. Realistically, why do most people download music? *To hear new music or records that have been deleted and are no longer available for purchase.* Not to avoid paying
40 $5 at the local used CD store or taping it off the radio, but to hear music they can't find anywhere else.

In the hysteria of the moment, everyone is forgetting the main way an artist becomes successful – *exposure*.

Without exposure, no one comes to shows, no one buys CDs, no one enables you to earn a living doing what you
45 love. Again, from personal experience: in 37 years as a recording artist, I've created 25+ albums for major labels, and I've *never once* received a royalty check that didn't show I owed *them* money. So I make most of my living from live touring, playing for 80–1,500 people a
50 night, doing my own show. I spend hours each week doing press, writing articles, making sure my website tour information is up to date. So when someone writes and tells me they came to my show because they'd downloaded a song and gotten curious, I am thrilled!
55

If you think about it, the music industry should be rejoicing at this new technological advance! Here's a fool-proof way to deliver music to millions who might otherwise never purchase a CD in a store. The cross-marketing opportunities are unbelievable. It's
60 instantaneous, costs are minimal, shipping non-existent … an obvious vehicle for higher earnings and lower costs. Instead, they're running around like chickens with their heads cut off, bleeding on everyone and making no sense.

There is *zero* evidence that material available for free online
65 downloading is financially harming anyone. In fact, most of the hard evidence is to the contrary. Please note that I am *not* arguing for indiscriminate downloading without the artist's permission. I am *not* saying copyrights are meaningless. I am objecting to the RIAA spin that they are
70 doing this to protect 'the artists' and make us more money. I am annoyed that so many records I once owned are out of print, and the only place I could find them was Napster*. Most of all, I'd like to see an end to the hysteria that causes a group like the RIAA to spend over 45 million dollars in
75 2001 lobbying 'on our behalf', when every record company out there is complaining that they have no money.

As artists, we have the ear of the masses. We have the trust of the masses. By speaking out in our concerts and in the press, we can do a great deal to calm this
80 hysteria, and put the blame for the sad state of our industry right back where it belongs – in the laps of record companies, radio programmers and our own apparent inability to organise ourselves in order to better our own lives – and those of our fans. If we don't
85 take charge, no one will.

* a file-sharing music website, now operating as a legal company

2 Answer these questions by choosing the correct letter, A, B, C or D.

1 Why does Janis Ian reject the views of the RIAA's focus groups? (paragraph 3)
   A She thinks the RIAA failed to invite enough people to take part.
   B She saw no supporting documentation from the RIAA about them.
   C She feels the groups only told the RIAA what they wanted to hear.
   D She heard that the RIAA had not run the exercise scientifically.

2 What does Janis Ian say about her website? (paragraph 4)
   A It has helped to promote her new hit record.
   B She is unable to include her own songs on it.
   C It has increased the sales of her recordings.
   D She is disappointed by the number of visitors.

3 How has Janis Ian been able to keep earning money as a musician? (paragraph 5)
   A thanks to her recording companies
   B due to how she publicises herself
   C because of large royalty checks
   D through touring with other bands

4 According to Janis Ian, the music industry should be positive about the Internet because (paragraph 6)
   A it has already reduced delivery charges.
   B it allows existing customers to be contacted.
   C it has provided better access to music stores.
   D it offers a completely different market.

5 Janis Ian is particularly angry with the music industry because (paragraph 7)
   A they have wasted money fighting the downloading issue.
   B they have not asked her for her permission.
   C they have not done enough to protect her sales.
   D they have deleted too many of her old recordings.

Grammar **G** ⋯⟩ STUDENT'S BOOK page 140

Concessive clauses

3 Complete the second sentence so that it means the same as the first, using the words in brackets.

1 Even though we appear to listen to more music nowadays, fewer of us learn to play an instrument. (despite)
   Nowadays, ... that we appear to listen to more music, fewer of us learn to play an instrument.

2 Although the singer Rod Stewart is in his 60s, he gave a solid live performance at last night's concert. (in spite of)
   .... in his 60s, the singer Rod Stewart gave a solid live performance at last night's concert.

3 Most artists are in favour of downloading, but the band Metallica are opposed to it. (whereas)
   Most artists see downloading as a good thing, ... not.

4 Despite having practised those chords a lot, I find them too difficult. (even though)
   I find those chords too difficult .... practised them a lot.

Vocabulary

4 Complete the table with related forms of the words given. The first five words have related forms in the second half of the article, and the rest revise words from the Student's Book.

Noun	Adjective	Adverb
realism		
	artistic	
technology		
finance		
		meaninglessly
effect		
	unpredictable	
universe		
		scientifically
	manipulative	

Writing Workout 2 on page 46 practises some of these words.

5 Write adjectives from the Student's Book (page 40) for the definitions given in brackets. Each adjective starts with the last letter of the adjective to its left and ends with the first letter of the one to its right.

EXAMPLE: OPTIMISTIC _c a r e f r e e_ ELATED
          (without any worries or problems)

1 MISERABLE _ _ _ _ _ _ _ DEPRESSED
   (unable to relax because of something pleasant that is going to happen)
2 BORING _ _ _ _ _ _ YOUNG
   (dark or unhappy)
3 IDIOSYNCRATIC _ _ _ _ _ _ _ _ LIVELY
   (happy and positive about life)
4 POWERFUL _ _ _ _ _ - _ _ _ _ _ _ _ DANGEROUS
   (entertaining or amusing, and not serious)
5 INNATE _ _ _ _ _ _ _ _ _ LOUD
   (having strong feelings)

Reading

1 Read this extract from a book about how babies explore the world around them. Time yourself as you read.

⏱ about 625 words

How babies think

The similarities between babies and scientists become particularly vivid when we consider how babies learn about things. In science, and even in ordinary life, we look beyond the surfaces of the world and try to infer its deeper patterns. We look for the underlying, hidden causes of events. We try to figure out the nature of things.

It's not just that we human beings *can* do this; we *need* to do it. We seem to have a kind of explanatory drive, like our drive for food. When we're presented with a puzzle, a mystery, a hint of a pattern, something that doesn't quite make sense, we work until we find a solution. In fact, we intentionally set ourselves such problems, like crossword puzzles, video games or detective stories. As scientists, we may stay up all night in the grip of a problem, even forgetting to eat, and it seems rather unlikely that our salaries are the sole motivation.

We see this same drive to understand the world in its purest form in children. Human children in the first three years of life are consumed by a desire to explore and experiment with objects. In fact, we take this for granted as a sometimes exhausting fact of parenting. We childproof our houses and say, with a sigh, that the baby is 'always getting into things'.

From the time human babies can move around, they are torn between the safety of a grown-up embrace and the irresistible drive to explore. Toddlers in the park seem attached to their mothers or fathers by invisible bungee cords: they venture out to explore and then, in a sudden panic, race back to the safe haven, only to venture forth again some few minutes later.

Seen from an evolutionary point of view, children's exploratory behaviour is rather peculiar. Not only do babies expend enormous energy in exploring the world, their explorations often endanger their very survival. The explanation seems to be that, for our species, the dangers of exploration are offset by the benefits of learning. The rapid and profound changes in children's understanding of the world seem related to the ways they explore and experiment. Children actively do things to promote their understanding of disappearances, causes and categories.

Fortunately, these aspects of the physical world are so ubiquitous that babies can do their experiments quite easily and for the most part safely. The cot, the house, the garden are excellent laboratories. For instance, we can see babies become interested in, almost obsessed with, hiding-and-finding games when they are about a year old. Babies also spontaneously carry out solo investigations of the mysterious Case of the Disappearing Object.

We once recorded a baby putting the same ring under a cloth and finding it 17 times in succession, saying 'all gone' each time. In our experiments, babies often begin by protesting when we take the toy to hide it. But after one or two turns, they often start hiding the toy themselves or give the cloth and toy to us with instructions to hide it again. Eighteen-month-olds, who are not renowned for their long attention span, will play this game for half an hour.

By the time babies are one or two years old, they will quite systematically explore the way one object can influence another object, for instance experimenting with using a rake to pull a toy towards them. The toy itself isn't nearly as interesting as the fact that the rake moves it closer.

A key aspect of our developmental picture is that babies are actively engaged in looking for patterns in what is going on around them, in testing hypotheses and in seeking explanations. They aren't just amorphous blobs that are stamped by evolution or shaped by their environment or moulded by adults.

2 Complete each sentence with the correct ending from the box. ⋯⟶ TF4

1 Crossword puzzles
2 Salaries
3 Parents
4 Young children
5 The benefits of learning
6 Children's experiments

A may try to prevent exploration.
B may compensate for the risks that exploration involves.
C show that our development is determined by evolution and environment.
D satisfy our need to look for explanations.
E may be ways of understanding relationships between objects.
F do not always demonstrate the value of exploration.
G are probably not an adequate reason for exploring.
H provide insight into successful ways to explore.
I may alternate attempts to explore with a return to safety.

3 Complete the summary below. Choose NO MORE THAN ONE WORD from the passage for each answer. ⋯⟶ TF10

Experiments by babies and young children

Babies use their surroundings as **1** .... where they can investigate the world, and their experiments – or games – can occupy their **2** .... for a surprisingly long time. One baby is reported to have repeated an experiment 17 times, using a **3** .... to hide a toy. Another common activity is for children to move a toy towards them with a **4** .... It is clear that babies and young children try to find **5** .... of what they see.

Vocabulary

4 The verbs in the box come from the reading passage. Complete the sentences below using the verbs in the correct form. Use each verb once only.

carry out   endanger   make   offset   promote   seek
shape   take   test   underlie

1 We generally .... it for granted that children will grow up with an understanding of the world around them, but we do not consider how this comes about.
2 A considerable amount of research has been .... into how babies learn that an object can still exist after it has disappeared.
3 Research usually involves first formulating a hypothesis and then .... it.
4 Television programmes about children do a great deal to .... understanding of their needs.
5 When something strange happens, we try to find an explanation that will .... sense of it.
6 Even after we have .... explanations of mysterious occurrences, we may not know their true cause.
7 Our genes and our environment help to .... our personalities.
8 A lack of opportunity to explore as a child may .... a person's weaknesses as an adult.
9 Babies may be .... by their efforts to explore their surroundings.
10 The cost of childproofing a home may be .... by the resulting reduction in damage.

Style Extra

It replacing a clause

5 Combine these pairs of sentences by making the first one the subject or object of the other, and using *it*. Make any other changes that are necessary.

EXAMPLE: Nearly every successful civilisation has been willing to explore. This has been noted.

It has been noted that nearly every successful civilisation has been willing to explore.

1 We are driven to ensure the success and continuation of not just our own genes, but of the species. This appears to be the case.
2 The Earth rotates on its axis once a day and travels round the sun once a year. This was asserted by Copernicus in 1530.
3 The planets orbit round the sun. Most people in the 16th century found this hard to believe.
4 A large comet or asteroid will hit the Earth. This is unlikely.
5 We have extended our knowledge of the universe. Radio telescopes have made this possible.
6 We will establish settlements on the moon. This will take a great deal of time, effort and money.

8 Culinary tools

Writing

1 This report is written rather informally and clumsily. Change the words and phrases in *italics* to make the style more formal. In some cases, it would be helpful to change the sentence structure. This will help you to write in a more academic style.

Kitchen of the Future Research Unit

To: Board of Directors
From: Director of Kitchen of the Future Research Unit
Subject: Future of the Unit
Date: 26 April

Terms of reference

This report is *meant* to highlight problems the Kitchen of the Future Research Unit now *has*.

Physical environment

The Unit is based in an annex of the company's head office. *But* the facilities are *old-fashioned*, and the offices are *messy, with lots of reports, equipment, etc. everywhere.* Staff *sometimes can't answer when someone asks for specific information,* as *they can't find* the relevant report. So *it's* likely that, unless the Unit moves to *a nicer building very soon, it won't be able to carry on working.*

Work of the Unit

The Unit *writes lots of* reports on innovations affecting the food industry. Reports are commissioned by outside bodies, and staff *go* anywhere in the world to *do* the necessary research. *They're so good* that they can produce a report in *no time at all.*

Staff also work on projects to invent new products, most recently the 'Music Knife', a gadget which *makes it easy to do preparations for cooking* by playing music of *the right* mood and speed.

Grammar **G**┄┄⟶ STUDENT'S BOOK page 140

Conditionals

2 These sentences come from comments made about various kitchen gadgets and small appliances. Complete each sentence with the correct ending from the box, using each ending once only. Think about both the meaning and the grammar.

1 You should buy an ice-cream maker
2 You'll have difficulty making good spaghetti in this pasta machine
3 I wouldn't give up my set of kitchen knives
4 I'd never have realised how useful a coffee machine can be
5 It isn't really necessary to buy kitchen scales
6 The pump of the coffee machine is likely to get damaged
7 Don't buy a pasta machine
8 Please don't expect me to use the espresso machine
9 I think this ice-cream maker would be easier to use
10 I'm sure my espresso machine would have gone on for years

A unless you like to be very accurate about measurements.
B if I hadn't been given one as a birthday present.
C unless you eat a lot of spaghetti.
D if you don't follow the instructions carefully.
E if the coffee you put in is too coarse.
F if the instructions were clearer.
G even if someone offered me twice what I paid for them.
H if you want to be able to make a lovely, creamy dessert very quickly.
I if I hadn't overheated the motor.
J unless someone cleans it for me each time.

Reading

3 Read this introduction to a report on sales of kitchen appliances. Time yourself as you read.

⏱ about 350 words

INTRODUCTION TO KITCHEN APPLIANCE REPORT UK

Growth continued in the market last year, although at a much lower rate than in previous years. The trend from free-standing towards built-in appliances is gathering pace. In the free-standing sector, growth
5 has mainly been concentrated at the upper end of the market, as an increasing proportion of consumers trade up to higher-specification appliances.

The major sector within built-in appliances is cooking (including microwaves) with 79% by volume. Within
10 the free-standing market, cooking takes 28% by volume, compared to refrigeration (31%), laundry (33%) and dishwashers (8%).

Built-in appliances

The built-in cooking market comprises ovens, hobs and
15 hoods. Many microwaves can be either built-in or free-standing.

The built-in oven sector is the largest by value. Although gas has made some gains in share in
20 recent years, the sector is primarily electric, estimated at 65%. Unlike ovens, the hob sector is predominantly gas, which accounts for around 59%, with electric hobs accounting for the balance. The built-in cooking
25 market has experienced considerable growth in terms of volume, and this has spread to increased demand for extractor hoods.

Refrigeration products are led by refrigerators, freezers and fridge/freezers.

Built-in dishwashers are still low in terms of
30 penetration, and growth potential still exists. They represent around 20% of the total dishwasher appliance market, a higher level than built-in refrigeration or laundry appliances.

Free-standing appliances

The free-standing cooking appliance market consists
35 of cookers and microwaves. Free-standing cookers comprise gas – with a 55% share – dual fuel and electric. The increasing trend towards larger cooking appliances has resulted in the growth of range cookers.
40

The free-standing refrigeration sector comprises refrigerators, freezers and fridge/freezers. The refrigeration market is saturated, with overall penetration at 99%. The trend towards larger appliances has resulted in significant growth within
45 the fridge/freezer sector.

There were some 934,000 free-standing dishwashers sold last year. Compared to other household appliances, the dishwasher market remains at a relatively low level of household penetration. The
50 wider product range, including slimline and compact dishwashers, and increased consumer awareness of the benefits the dishwasher can offer, have contributed to growth in this sector.

---

4 Do the following statements agree with the information given in the text? ⋯⟶ TF2

Write

TRUE   *if the statement agrees with the information*

FALSE   *if the statement contradicts the information*

NOT GIVEN   *if there is no information on this*

1 Purchasers of free-standing appliances are tending to buy cheaper models.

2 Cooking appliances account for a higher proportion of built-in appliances than of free-standing ones.

3 Among built-in ovens, the proportion of gas ovens has grown.

4 In the built-in sector, more electric ovens were sold than gas hobs.

5 Sales of extractor hoods have been affected by trends in sales of cooking appliances.

6 The proportion of people with built-in dishwashers is at its highest possible level.

7 Sales of free-standing gas cookers are rising.

8 Most free-standing range cookers use gas.

9 The relative proportions of refrigerators, freezers and fridge/freezers being sold are static.

10 Sales of dishwashers have been influenced by an increase in the number of types of dishwasher available.

9 Old and new

Reading

1 Read this passage about transport in Bogotá. Time yourself as you read.

⏱ about 450 words

THE WORLD LEARNS FROM BOGOTÁ

At a recent international urban planning conference, the International Seminar on Human Mobility, delegates from 38 nations took tours of pedestrian-friendly boulevards in this city of 9 million
5   inhabitants. They also participated in Bogotá's 'ciclovia': every Sunday, 120 kilometres of streets are closed to traffic, and around two million residents jog, skate or bike around their city.

'I wonder if we could do this in Buenos Aires,'
10 said a wide-eyed Horacio Blot, a government transport co-ordinator in that city, as he observed the bicycles, buses and taxis that Bogotá's residents use to commute to work and school on the city's Car-Free Day, the largest of its kind in the world.
15 Ministers of transport, mayors of capital cities and representatives from NGOs met at the event to observe first-hand the transformation of the Colombian capital, which has gone from being one of the most dangerous, traffic-ensnarled and polluted
20 cities to a model for urban transport and social policy. Delegates learned about varied topics, such as Misión Bogotá, a programme whereby marginalised citizens and petty criminals are given jobs directing bicycle traffic or transit users, bike paths in Lima and
25 plans to build a subway in Tehran. Bogotá's current mayor explained how he managed to reduce homicide by a staggering 40% in 1996 by closing nightclubs at 1 a.m.

From 1998 to 2000, under the city's former mayor
30 Enrique Peñalosa, many resident-friendly initiatives were successfully undertaken. Not only did the city construct the largest network of bicycle paths in the developing world (270 kilometres' worth), it also introduced an extensive bus rapid-transit system
35 called TransMilenio, which has helped to reduce automobile use by 40% during peak times. Construction of the stunning municipal library that hosted the conference also began under Peñalosa, as part of his effort to provide high-quality public space
40 to all of the city's residents.

Conference visits were organised to experience the TransMilenio. This highly efficient 'surface subway' moves 770,000 passengers at a low cost, making it an obvious choice for developing countries, which have huge transport needs and limited funds. Lawrence   45
Kumi, transport minister of Ghana, said 'We are thinking seriously of applying the TransMilenio model in Accra.' Michael Replogle of the United States NGO Environmental Defense said, 'While I have long advocated bus rapid-transit strategies,   50
seeing how effectively Bogotá has implemented them through TransMilenio was a real eye-opener. Bogotá's success in changing its infrastructure to become much more bicycle and pedestrian friendly in a short span of time is most impressive and provides an   55
inspiring model to other cities around the world.' So it seems that many countries could learn a lot from Bogotá's example of urban planning.

2 Decide whether the following statements accurately reflect the content of the passage. Write T (true) or F (false), and underline the words in the passage that provide the answer. ⋯⋗ TF2

1 Horacio Blot was impressed by Bogotá's Car-Free Day.
2 Members of various national governments attended the conference.
3 People with a criminal record are ineligible to work on the Misión Bogotá programme.
4 The murder rate in the city was cut significantly during the 1990s.
5 Building work on the city library was completed during Enrique Peñalosa's term of office.
6 Solely as a result of the conference, Michael Replogle is now convinced of the value of bus rapid-transit systems.

3 Tick (✓) any of the following aspects that are covered by the passage. If no information is given, write *NG*.

1 streets that are uncrossable
2 a regular traffic-free programme
3 previous congestion in the city
4 a similar cycling project in another country
5 plans to extend the TransMilenio
6 the throughput of passengers of the TransMilenio

Vocabulary

4 The passage contains the expressions *wide-eyed* and *a real eye-opener*, which are to do with observation and revelation. Match the expressions in italics with the verbs (a–h).

1 I wanted to *see with my own eyes* what the city had achieved.
2 Stephen Knight never *saw eye to eye* with his colleagues in the planning department and eventually decided to resign.
3 The gallery's stunning glass-and-steel entrance *catches the eye* as you go in.
4 Carla's mother will always regret *turning a blind eye* to her daughter's problems.
5 You need to get an experienced chemist to *cast an eye over* your dissertation before you hand it in.
6 Hilary had never *laid eyes on* the place before, but it immediately felt like home.
7 There's a lot more to this news report *than meets the eye* – the city council must be engaged in a cover-up.
8 Could you *keep an eye on* my bags for a moment while I go and buy a paper?

a check
b ignore
c agree
d guard, look after
e observe first-hand
f attract attention
g see
h be more complicated

Writing

5 Use the linkers in the box to complete the summary of the conference in Bogotá.

a third	alongside	among	another
but also	not only	one	thus

Many of the delegates found the conference a very positive experience. **1** .... was going to consider implementing a traffic-free day in his own city; **2** .... wanted to use the TransMilenio as a model; **3** .... was visibly impressed, **4** .... by how much had been achieved in Bogotá, **5** .... how quickly the infrastructure had been improved. **6** .... the former mayor's achievements were the city's cycle network and the TransMilenio. **7** .... these projects, Peñalosa also initiated the building of the new library. It is **8** .... that Bogotá has been transformed into one of the most resident-friendly cities in the whole world.

Grammar Ⓖ ⋯⋗ STUDENT'S BOOK page 140

Inversion of adverbs

6 Rewrite the sentences without the inversion of the adverb.

EXAMPLE: Hardly could the gallery cope with the sudden influx of visitors.

The gallery could hardly cope with the sudden influx of visitors.

1 Scarcely could Ben have known about the road closures as he doesn't drive.
2 No sooner had the traffic lights turned green before they went back to red again.
3 Rarely have I visited as beautiful a city as Ljubljana, the capital of Slovenia.
4 Hardly need I add that all mobile phones should now be switched off.
5 Barely was there enough room for everyone who boarded the bus.

In your dreams

Reading

1 Read this article quickly without stopping, timing yourself as you read. Then read it again, stopping at each underlined word or phrase to check meaning in a dictionary, if necessary.

⏱ about 750 words

The selling of the Senoi

Ever since the 1930s, through the writings of the American psychologist Kilton Stewart and others, a great deal of interest has been generated in the Senoi tribe, from whom, it has been suggested, the West might learn the art of self-
5 *improvement through dream manipulation. Ann Faraday and John Wren-Lewis spent over a year living with the Senoi in a remote region of Malaysia, in order to research the precise role of dreams in Senoi culture. As a result, Faraday and Wren-Lewis have become fiercely critical of what they see as*
10 *a misrepresentation of Senoi beliefs. Here is an extract from what they wrote following their period of field research.*

It would be hard to imagine a people more dedicated to preserving their traditions intact, despite all the changes going on around them. We spent night after night listening to
15 tales of olden days or joining in their frequent trance/dance sessions in which dream-inspired songs are used to call spirits, and our welcome would have been short-lived had we not <u>scrupulously</u> observed their time-hallowed rituals and taboos. We made a special point of talking to elders who
20 could recall the 1930s, and one of them, who actually told his dreams to Noone and Stewart, became a key <u>informant</u> in our investigations. We also sought out the dreamers named by Stewart in his PhD thesis, finding two of them still living and interviewing the families of others.

25 Sadly, we must report that no one recalled any form of dream-control education in childhood or any such practice amongst adults; in fact, they <u>vehemently denied</u> that dream manipulation has ever been part of their culture. Given that dreams play such an integral part in their whole religious life,
30 we cannot conceive of a major dream-practice being allowed to <u>fade into oblivion</u> when the religion itself is so very much alive. There is an elaborate Temiar lore for interpreting dreams as warnings or omens (though only the shaman's interpretations have ever been given serious credence), and
35 great attention has always been paid to anyone receiving a song or dance in dreams, for this indicates the emergence of a new shaman to <u>invoke</u> spirits for healing or protection of the village.

However, no one, absolutely no one, would ever have
40 presumed to ask for, still less demand, such a gift from a dream-character, as Western 'Senoi dream theory' advocates.

The Cameron Highlands region, Malaysia

This would be high heresy for Temiar religion, in which the 'gunig', or protective spirit, always chooses its human vehicle and would be repelled by any hint of coercion; in fact, the Temiar abhor <u>coercion</u> of any kind, dreaming or waking. They 45 dismiss as nonsense the idea that children can be trained to confront hostile dream-characters, and <u>boggle</u> at the idea of converting such a figure into a gunig by fighting or killing it.

Another point we took special pains to probe was whether Temiar culture had ever given any place to what is now in the 50 West called dream lucidity, awareness within a dream that one is dreaming. We framed our questions very carefully (an essential precaution in any investigation like this) and were interested to find that many Temiars, and notably all our shaman informants, understood at once what we were asking. 55 In other words, they had no difficulty in grasping that one might have such awareness in a dream – but they <u>emphatically denied</u> that it played any part in their tradition.

As more and more evidence along these lines reaches Western literature (and there is plenty more still to come), we 60 feel we must put a ban on the misuse of their name, which proponents of dream control seem reluctant to do. Just enclosing the word 'Senoi' in inverted commas isn't good enough, for the real Senoi have a real dream culture of which they are very proud, and they become quite indignant when 65 they hear their name identified with concepts utterly alien from their own. Some smart leaders even suggested to us that their newly formed tribal association could sue, or perhaps insist on a royalty from every book or workshop that takes their name in vain! Meanwhile, writings are already in 70 the pipeline, from ourselves and others, which will bring real Senoi dream culture firmly into Western literature, so nothing but confusion can come from retaining the name for psychological techniques invented in America.

2 Answer these questions by choosing the correct letter, A, B, C or D. ⟶ TF5

1 When Faraday and Wren-Lewis stayed with the Senoi, they
   A decided to observe dancing rather than take part in it.
   B were unable to locate any participants in the 1930s fieldwork.
   C felt saddened by the effects of modernisation on the people.
   D were careful to follow the social code of the tribe strictly.

2 According to Faraday and Wren-Lewis, Senoi dream manipulation
   A is only practised in adulthood.
   B is now a forgotten ritual.
   C is just a myth created by Stewart.
   D is something you are born with.

3 Faraday and Wren-Lewis suggest that, for the Senoi, a 'gunig'
   A might on occasion seek human help.
   B would welcome requests for inspiration.
   C could once have been a dream-character.
   D will select every shaman unaided.

4 What is the Senoi attitude to 'dream lucidity'?
   A They cannot comprehend the concept.
   B It has never been one of their customs.
   C They don't recognise it as a possibility.
   D It is relevant to their dream culture.

5 Why do Faraday and Wren-Lewis request a ban on using the name 'Senoi'?
   A because the Senoi way of life has been seriously misrepresented
   B because members of the tribe have threatened them with legal action
   C because otherwise book royalties will have to be paid to the Senoi
   D because no American since Stewart has ever visited the tribe

Vocabulary

3 Read the clues and complete the crossword. The number of letters is given in brackets. All the words can be found in the passage.

Across
1 The control of something (12)
3 Exact or accurate (7)
7 The traditional stories of a country or culture (4)
8 Actions or words that are avoided in a particular culture (6)
11 Someone's position or function in a society (4)
13 A person who has special healing and spiritual powers (6)
14 An ethnic group, such as the Senoi (5)
15 A belief or action that is against generally accepted beliefs (6)

Down
2 Someone who is interviewed by field researchers (9)
4 A way of behaving according to traditions or customs (6)
5 Forcefully (indicating very strong feelings) (10)
6 Decide on the meaning or significance of something (9)
9 Something that indicates what is likely to happen in the future (4)
10 A state of mind where someone appears to have no conscious control in spite of being awake (6)
12 A story (4)

Grammar **G** ⟶ STUDENT'S BOOK page 141

Modal verbs

4 Rewrite these sentences as questions, using modal verbs.

EXAMPLE: The recurring images of snow might indicate your uncertainty.

Might *the recurring images of snow indicate your uncertainty?*

The recurring images of snow *might indicate your uncertainty*, mightn't they?

1 My bad dream last night could have been due to that cheese I ate.
   Could .... ?
   .... , could it?

2 Your inability to remember your dreams could be reversible.
   The fact that you ....
   .... , mightn't it?
   Mightn't .... ?

3 It's impossible that David's dream was caused by watching that film.
   David's dream ....
   ....
   There's no way that ....
   ....

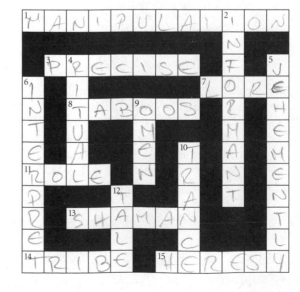

The physical world

Reading

1 Read this article, timing yourself as you read.

⏱ about 400 words

The Santorini volcano

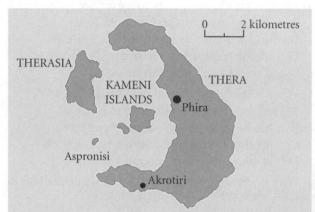

A Santorini is a small cluster of islands in the Aegean Sea, or eastern Mediterranean, just over 100 kilometres north of the much larger island of Crete. Once a single, circular mass, the centre of the
5 island has fallen into the sea, leaving a rough ring consisting of Thera, the crescent-shaped main island, and some smaller islands.

B About two million years ago, lava – liquid rock from the magma below the Earth's crust – began to be
10 forced out of vents in the area of the present-day Akrotiri peninsula in the south of Thera. Over the last 200,000 years, the island has experienced a cycle in which the creation of volcanoes from lava has alternated with large explosive eruptions, of
15 which there have been at least 12 in this period.

C Excavations on Akrotiri have uncovered evidence of habitation going back over 5,000 years. 3,800 years ago, the town was a prosperous seaport of the Minoan people, whose civilisation – centred on
20 Crete – covered a large area of the eastern Mediterranean. Akrotiri was one of the main urban centres and ports of the Aegean. It had a population of about 30,000, an elaborate drainage system and sophisticated buildings, some of them
25 two and even three storeys high, containing wall paintings and furniture.

D About 3,650 years ago, the volcano erupted and hurled 30 to 40 cubic kilometres of magma – hot, liquid rock – into the air, in a column reaching a height of 36 kilometres above the island. With so 30 much magma removed, the volcano, and the entire centre of the island, collapsed into the sea, producing the largest crater on Earth. Ash was blown eastwards, and fell over a large area of the eastern Mediterranean and Turkey, probably with a 35 global impact on the climate. On Santorini itself, pumice and ash were deposited in layers up to 50 metres thick, and Akrotiri was buried under one to two metres of ash. Tidal waves swept south to Crete. This eruption is thought to have brought the 40 Minoan civilisation to an abrupt end.

E Fortunately, the residents appear to have been successfully evacuated prior to the eruption, as no bodies or movable objects have been found in the ash. There is speculation that it was the destruction 45 of this town that gave rise to the legend of the disastrous flood which engulfed the island nation of Atlantis.

2 Choose the correct heading for each paragraph (A–E) from the list of headings in the box (i–viii).
···⟩ TF1

> **List of Headings**
>   **i** Lives saved – and a mythological link
> **ii** How homes were constructed
> **iii** Santorini today
> **iv** A legend proved true
>   **v** How Santorini was destroyed
> **vi** A wealthy settlement
> **vii** Links with volcanic eruptions elsewhere
> **viii** A history of volcanic activity

1 Paragraph A: ....
2 Paragraph B: ....
3 Paragraph C: ....
4 Paragraph D: ....
5 Paragraph E: ....

Vocabulary

3 The use of noun phrases rather than verbs is common in academic writing. Complete the second sentences below with a phrase of no more than four words, so that they mean roughly the same as the first sentences. Each phrase should contain a noun that is related to a verb in the first sentence.

EXAMPLE: The volcano erupted about 3,650 years ago, and this may have led to the end of the Minoan civilisation.

The *eruption of the volcano* about 3,650 years ago may have led to the end of the Minoan civilisation.

1 The volcano collapsed and this created a large crater.
The .... created a large crater.
2 The residents were evacuated, and their lives were saved.
The .... saved their lives.
3 Akrotiri was destroyed, and this may have given rise to the Atlantis legend.
The .... may have given rise to the Atlantis legend.
4 There is evidence that Santorini was inhabited 5,000 years ago.
There is .... on Santorini 5,000 years ago.
5 Some people have speculated that the destruction of Akrotiri gave rise to the Atlantis legend.
There has been .... that the destruction of Akrotiri gave rise to the Atlantis legend.
6 Akrotiri was prosperous and this resulted from its importance for trade.
.... resulted from its importance for trade.

4 Complete these sentences with adjectives from the box, using each adjective once only. The adjective-noun collocations are based on the reading passage on page 74 of the Student's Book.

> compelling   full-blown   fundamental
> physical   scientific

1 Faced with .... new evidence, scientists accepted that the Earth revolves round the sun.
2 The .... community is sometimes taken in by deliberate lies and tricks.
3 Einstein's findings raised .... questions about the nature of time and space.
4 For centuries, movement of the continents was thought to be a .... impossibility.
5 Scientists often spend years carrying out research before presenting a .... theory.

Grammar Ⓖ ···⟩ STUDENT'S BOOK page 141

Non-finite clauses

5 Put the verbs in brackets into the correct non-finite form (e.g. *to do*, *doing* or *done*).

1 (situate) .... in the Aegean Sea, Santorini is not far from Crete.
2 Excavations have uncovered evidence of habitation (date) .... back over 5,000 years.
3 The Minoan civilisation, (base) .... in Crete, covered much of the eastern Mediterranean.
4 For the standard of living in Akrotiri (meet) .... the needs of a population of 30,000, drainage was introduced.
5 The centre of the island collapsed, (leave) .... a circle of land around a crater.
6 One reason for excavating at Akrotiri is (find) .... evidence of the earliest habitation.
7 Many people believe Atlantis (be) .... a legend based on the eruption at Santorini.

6 Underline the 11 non-finite verbs in the passage about Santorini. There are six *-ing* forms, two *-ed* forms and three infinitives. Don't underline non-finite forms that are part of finite verbs, such as *(has) experienced* (line 12) or adjectives like *sophisticated* (line 24).

Nature or nurture?

Reading

1 Read this magazine article, timing yourself as you read.

⏱ about 450 words

'Wisdom and knowledge reside in Timbuktu'
(old West African proverb)

A 900 years ago, in the 12th century, Timbuktu was becoming one of the great centres of learning in the Islamic world. Scholars and students travelled from as far away as Cairo, Baghdad and Persia to study from the noted manuscripts found in the town. Respected scholars who taught in Timbuktu were referred to throughout North Africa as 'ambassadors of peace'.

B An integral part of Timbuktu's history was always trade – the exchange of salt that came from the heart of the Sahara. To this day, camel caravans laden with salt, also known as 'the gold of the desert', journey to Timbuktu, in present-day Mali, West Africa, where the salt is sold in the markets of the Niger River towns of Mopti, Djénné and beyond.

C Accompanying the camel caravans rode the scholars of Islamic learning, bringing with them over the centuries hundreds of thousands of manuscripts. These bound texts highlighted the great teachings of Islam during the Middle Ages, on an array of subjects: astronomy, medicine, mathematics, chemistry, judicial law, government and Islamic conflict resolution. During this period of human history, when intellectual evolution was virtually at a standstill in most of Europe, within the Muslim world Islamic study was growing, evolving and breaking new ground in the fields of science, mathematics, astronomy, law and philosophy.

D By the 1300s, the 'ambassadors of peace' centred around the University of Timbuktu created scholastic campuses and religious schools of learning that travelled between the cities of Timbuktu, Gao and Djénné, helping to serve as a model of peaceful governance throughout a region that was often the scene of tribal conflict. At its peak, over 25,000 students attended the University of Timbuktu.

E By the beginning of the 1600s, however, partly because of invasions, the scholars of Timbuktu had slowly begun to drift away and study elsewhere. As a result, the city's sacred manuscripts started to fall into disrepair. While Islamic teaching there continued for another 300 years, scholastic study fell off sharply with the French colonisation of the region in the late 1890s.

F In mud homes down sand-filled alleyways lie private collections of sacred manuscripts that date back hundreds of years. The Ahmed Baba Research Centre houses the largest collection. Some scholars estimate that there are over 700,000 manuscripts housed in numerous collections in Timbuktu.

G With the pressures of poverty and a series of droughts, many manuscripts have been sold illegally to private collectors abroad. However, through the efforts of the Timbuktu Heritage Institute, the manuscripts of Timbuktu are beginning to be re-catalogued, preserved and protected against theft.

H Today, Timbuktu, designated a World Heritage Site by the United Nations Education, Scientific and Cultural Organisation (UNESCO), lies at a crossroads. Its rich legacy of sacred manuscripts could possess a treasure chest of African history.

2 Which paragraph (A–H) contains the following information? You may use any letter more than once. ···⫶ TF8

   1 the fields of knowledge covered by the manuscripts
   2 a reference to conservation work being carried out on the manuscripts
   3 where Timbuktu is located
   4 an explanation of why some manuscripts are no longer in Timbuktu
   5 evidence of the spread of Timbuktu's fame to a distance
   6 an explanation of Timbuktu's economic importance
   7 an account of Timbuktu's decline as a centre of learning
   8 how the manuscripts reached Timbuktu

3 Complete these sentences with words taken from the passage. Use **NO MORE THAN THREE WORDS** for each answer. ···⫶ TF4

   1 In the Middle Ages, people came to study under the .... of Timbuktu.
   2 Merchants transport salt to Timbuktu in ....
   3 As scholars left, there was nobody to rescue the manuscripts from a state of ....
   4 Many private collections of manuscripts are to be found in .... in the town.
   5 The .... is responsible for the conservation of the manuscripts.
   6 Timbuktu has been classified as a ....

Grammar   Ⓖ ···⫶ STUDENT'S BOOK page 141

Infinitives

4 Choose from these infinitives for the verbs in brackets.

Active: to be doing	**Passive:** to be done
to have done	to have been done
to have been doing	

   1 Good musicians are often thought (inherit) .... their talent.
   2 It remains (see) .... whether my theory will be proved right.
   3 I'm sorry not (have) .... the chance to spend more time with you while you were on the course.
   4 The research team hopes (complete) .... the first stage of its study before the end of term.
   5 The situation seems (improve) .... even as we speak.
   6 Some birds lead people away from their nests because they do not want their chicks (find) ....
   7 This photograph is thought (take) .... in the 19th century.
   8 I would like (remember) .... as the inventor of something really useful.
   9 The injured man is thought (walk) .... past the factory when he was hit by a falling roof tile.
  10 The festival programme has just been published, and all sorts of exciting events seem (happen) ....

Vocabulary

5 Complete each sentence (1–8) with the most suitable ending (a–h). Use each ending once only. Make sure you understand the phrasal verbs, and notice the position of *on*.

   1 One of the biggest companies in my town is planning to
   2 If you get any further information, I'd be grateful if you would
   3 Sometimes when you aren't consciously thinking about a problem, you suddenly
   4 If we compare the costs of each proposal, it will help us to
   5 Before we get down to the main topic of discussion, I'd just like to
   6 The attendees will need refreshments during the meeting, so we'd better
   7 If you'd like to hear a simultaneous translation,
   8 Some students don't like it if their teachers

   a decide on the best one.
   b put your earphones on now.
   c pass it on to me.
   d lay them on in the adjoining room.
   e hit on a way of solving it.
   f take on several new trainees.
   g touch on one other point that isn't on the agenda.
   h check up on their attendance.

6 Which two endings in exercise 5 could have the particles in a different position?

Cosmic debris

Reading

1 Read this article about a potential asteroid impact with Earth. Time yourself as you read.

⏱ about 550 words

TOO CLOSE FOR COMFORT

The night of 13 April 2029 will be pretty special, because of what will probably be the closest near miss by a dangerous asteroid for over a millennium. It will be exceptionally close, with latest estimates putting the asteroid's proximity at around 25,600 kilometres from Earth's surface. If you are in Europe, Africa or Central Asia on the night it passes, asteroid 2004 MN4 will appear as a fairly bright star moving slowly across the sky.

MN4 was discovered in June 2004 and led to a few nail-biting days for astronomers later that year, when NASA's webpage on asteroid impact hazards gave this object the highest ever odds of hitting the Earth, more than 1 in 50 (although this later proved to be a false alarm). At around 300 metres across, the asteroid is capable of devastating a large city, making it one of this century's most serious dangers.

When an asteroid comes very close to a planet, gravity very slightly changes its orbit and speeds it up. This phenomenon has been the basis for many of the unmanned space missions over the last few decades, with a few 'gravity-assist' fly-bys included on the flight plan to speed probes on their way to outer space. However, until recently, no one had thought through the implications for asteroids.

Even though we now know that MN4 will miss us in 2029, it has a greater chance of hitting Earth later in the century, with various impact dates currently being predicted. These possible impacts are considered dangerous enough to be given a 1 on the Torino scale. This scale is an attempt to quantify the likelihood of potential impacts, with a rating of 0 indicating harmless and 10 signifying a certain impact, capable of causing a global catastrophe. In December 2004, MN4 was briefly given a rating of 4, albeit due to inaccurate calculations.

MN4 will be coming fairly close to Earth again soon, providing an opportunity for fresh observations. If these still show the possibility of future impacts, it might be a good idea to do something about it. The first thing would be to try to pin down MN4's exact position, and the best way to do that would apparently be to fix something such as a radio transponder to it. Such a project would incidentally give us a much better idea of the internal structure of asteroids. At the moment, we don't really know whether they are mostly solid, riddled with cracks or holes, or made up of lots of loose material.

The Hollywood-style assumption that hitting an asteroid with missiles is the only way of avoiding global catastrophe might in fact just lead to multiple Earth impacts, caused by its shattered remains. Instead, it may be preferable to simply push the troublesome asteroid gently aside. Strange as it may sound, one way to do this might be to spray the whole asteroid with white paint! The outcome of this would be to increase reflectance, and in so doing, alter the gravitational effects of solar radiation, leading the asteroid to drift gradually off course, and further away from Earth.

There may be no cinematic attraction in watching paint dry, but this option could just be the perfect solution. Only time will tell.

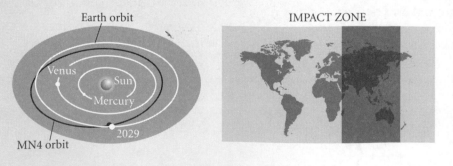

Earth orbit

Venus · Sun · Mercury

2029

MN4 orbit

IMPACT ZONE

RELATIVE SIZE OF MN4 TO DINOSAUR EXTINCTION ASTEROID

MN4

2 Complete the summary with words from the box. You will not need all the words.

> action ~~collision~~ controversy core
> data ~~destruction~~ ~~device~~ ~~effect~~
> eradication force ~~hypothesis~~ incidents
> nature research result risk shift
> ~~suggestion~~ termination

We will narrowly escape a **1** .... between asteroid MN4 and the Earth in 2029, and the chances of further catastrophic incidents are likely to increase during the century. If it ever does hit the Earth, the **2** .... caused by MN4 could affect an entire city, which is why astronomers are keen to conduct **3** .... on the asteroid in the very near future. One **4** .... which has already been made is to attach a radio **5** .... to the asteroid, which would give scientists a lot of valuable **6** .... on the precise **7** .... of the asteroid's **8** .... As far as preventing a future catastrophe, the **9** .... of detonating explosives on the asteroid is perceived to be unacceptable. This course of **10** .... might indeed have the opposite **11** .... to the one intended, triggering several simultaneous Earth impacts. A more promising idea is to promote a slight **12** .... in the asteroid's course by coating it with white paint. As a **13** .... , MN4 would reflect more of the sun's rays, and this would alter the **14** .... of gravity upon it, causing the asteroid to move away from its dangerous path.

Grammar **G**⋯⋰ STUDENT'S BOOK page 141

Future tenses

3 Put the verbs in brackets into a suitable simple or continuous future tense, using a negative or passive form where necessary. It may help you to refer back to the text opposite.

EXAMPLE: Asteroid MN4 (not/collide)
....._won't collide_..... with Earth in 2029.

1 However, it (pass) .... very near to our planet at that time.
2 The asteroid (affect) .... by its close encounter with Earth.

3 The speed at which MN4 (travel) .... after its fly-by of Earth (remain) .... constant, due to gravitational force.
4 Much (learn) .... about the internal structure of asteroids if the radio transponder mission goes ahead.
5 It (never/be) .... feasible to target the asteroid with missiles.
6 Should it be possible to increase MN4's reflectance, its trajectory (alter) .... and the threat to Earth diminished.

Vocabulary

4 Scan the text to find words meaning the same as 2–7 below. Use them to complete the word puzzle. What word from the text is revealed horizontally?

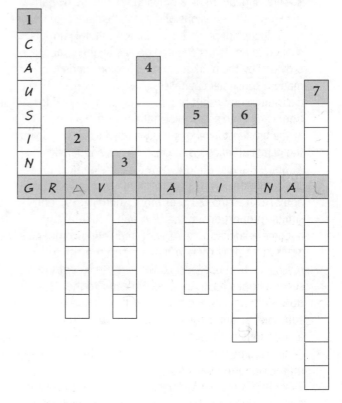

1 leading to
2 dangers
3 collision or force of one object hitting another
4 path through which an object moves around a planet
5 result
6 nearness
7 likely effects of an action

Trends in society

Reading

1 Read this Australian article about downshifting, where a person rejects a
highly paid job for a less stressful existence. Time yourself as you read.

⏱ about 575 words

The Social Implications
of Downshifting

Downshifting, with its emphasis on a better quality of
life, appears to be a growing trend in many parts of
the world. The decisions of downshifters are taken under
the influence of powerful social and cultural currents,
5 shaped to an unprecedented degree by the symbols
provided by the market and the ideology underlying
modern consumer capitalism. Evidence suggests that the
decision to downshift requires a process of untying oneself
from overriding social expectations, which are manifested
10 at the broadest level of society and which seep down to
the personal reactions of close friends and family.

Since downshifting is now such a significant
phenomenon – it is a choice made by nearly a quarter of
adult Australians (23% of those aged 30–59), and
15 similar proportions in the USA and Britain – it has
become a social force. Already, marketing companies are
advising their clients on how best to pitch their
messages to these 'anti-consumers'. In recent years,
several books have appeared to cater to the
20 downshifting trend, mostly 'how to' manuals, but also
some penetrating social analysis. Downshifting is not yet
a conscious political force, although the shift in priorities
of this segment of the electorate must be beginning to
influence voting patterns.

25 Perhaps before it becomes a political force, the social
critique adhered to by most downshifters, whether
explicitly or after some consideration, will need to be
debated more widely. There is no doubt that aspects of this
critique are widely held in the community amongst those
30 who have not contemplated downshifting. For example,
83% of Australians agree that their society is too
materialistic, with too much emphasis on money and not
enough on the things that really matter (Hamilton 2002).

In a world where we are unconsciously, or semi-
35 consciously, influenced by powerful forces to behave and
think of ourselves in certain ways, living more
consciously is a radical act. It is clear from the research
that for most downshifters, the change is one which
involves taking control of one's life and living more
consciously, and that making the change takes courage. 40
This is paradoxical in a society that celebrates individual
freedom and which, over the last two decades, has been
dominated by the modern politics of neoliberalism that
places so much importance on consumer choice. Why
does it take an act of courage to choose to devote less 45
time to earning money and acquiring things and more
time to other pursuits?

If people today are the authors of their own lives,
why do they hesitate for so long before writing the next
chapter? The answer is that, despite all of the rhetoric, 50
only certain forms of choice are socially permissible,
those that are consistent with acquisitiveness and the
desire to get on. The result, as we have found, is that
downshifters often lose friends and lose status, and their
relationship to society changes, sometimes in a 55
fundamental way. This is why it takes courage to decide
to work less or take a lower-paying job. At the same
time, downshifters often forge stronger friendships with
supportive others and create lives that, for them, are
more autonomous and fulfilling. 60

It appears that downshifters are increasingly willing
to defend their lifestyle choices, suggesting that soon,
downshifting will no longer be seen to be an act of
defiance. The decision to downshift will become
commonplace rather than a daring or atypical choice. At 65
that point, we will know that modern consumer society
has undergone a far-reaching change.

2 **Complete the sentences below. Choose NO MORE THAN TWO WORDS from the passage for each answer.**

1 Downshifting involves the individual concerned in a form of withdrawal from the .... that pervade all strata of modern life.

2 The current volume of people opting to downshift in Australia and elsewhere makes it a numerically ....

3 It is inevitable that the decision to downshift and consequent lifestyle changes will have an impact on the .... of those concerned.

4 Downshifting challenges society's preoccupation with .... and its recent elevation in importance.

5 One negative aspect of downshifting is that the individual's .... may be diminished.

Vocabulary

3 **Find adjectives in the passage that mean the following.**

1 exceptional (has never happened before) (paragraph 1)
2 predominant (paragraph 1)
3 deep (paragraph 2)
4 acquisitive (wanting new possessions) (paragraph 3)
5 extreme (paragraph 4)
6 deep and basic (paragraph 5)
7 independent (paragraph 5)
8 unusual (paragraph 6)

4 **Match the sets of nouns below to six of the adjectives you found in exercise 3. Every noun in the set must collocate with the adjective.**

1 concern   flaw   principle   problem
2 ideas   research   scream   stare
3 personality   reaction   response   results
4 arguments   considerations   factor   reason
5 views   politics   approach   solution
6 body   region   employees   state

Grammar G ···⟶ STUDENT'S BOOK page 142

Pronouns

5 **Insert the missing pronouns in these sentences written by IELTS candidates.**

1 When we exercise, we know that is difficult to avoid such a situation.

2 There are a lot more questions that we require answers to before can reach a verdict on such an important issue.

3 Finally, good relationships with the people around is another factor in how far we achieve happiness.

4 Rich countries should take more responsibility for helping the poorer.

5 Maybe for other people these things are not so important, but for me are very important.

6 In my essay, discuss the merits and demerits of the mobile phone.

7 Considering that Australia is a good place for jobs, is quite an alarming trend.

6 **Circle the correct pronouns.**

1 *Every / All* aspects of the case are once again subject to scrutiny, *which / what* may affect previous decisions.

2 The two politicians stared at *another / each other* in disbelief.

3 I forced *myself / me* to study one more chapter before bedtime.

4 There is a noticeable difference between your interpretation of the law and *ours / our*.

5 Most people, no matter *who / whoever* they are, abhor violent behaviour.

6 There must be an explanation for *whose / these* declining standards *somewhere / anywhere* in this paper.

7 Even if your lifestyle becomes slower and simpler, *they / it* need not be less fun.

8 There were only a few applicants for the post, and most of *those / they* weren't suitable.

9 Two separate reasons have been given for the anomaly, but *either / neither* seems remotely plausible to me.

10 My first English teacher is *anyone / someone* for *who / whom* I still have a lot of respect.

Risk and reality

Reading

1   Read this passage, timing yourself as you read.

⏱ about 600 words

Exploring the nature of illness

This website is designed to explore how the experience, diagnosis and treatment of illness has changed over time, and to show some of the many ways illness has been understood by humans. Several questions are explored: How has medical
5   practice changed over time? How is medicine related to culture? How have names for illness changed over time? How does viewing our own medical practices from a historical perspective change how we understand our current, familiar practices? It is our hope that you will leave the site with a
10   broader appreciation of the relationship of medicine to culture, and an understanding that our own medical practices look different when seen in a historical context.

In exploring this site, we ask you to grapple with a fundamental, radical idea: that illness, the feeling and
15   experience of being sick, is itself a historical object. Illness and medicine are not static phenomena. Different people in different time periods can experience, understand and treat similar groups of symptoms very differently. Cycles of fevers and chills may be identified as being a particular disease, part
20   of a general pattern of seasonal health or an internal struggle of opposing yet complementary forces. These are more than just descriptions; they influence the actual experience of having illness, and strongly influence the treatment. A body that is out of balance feels pain in a manner that is
25   subjectively different from a body fighting a battle against an external attacker. We believe that illness changes over time. Thus, to fully understand illness, we need not just biological explanations, but also historical explanations. We need both medicine and the history of medicine.
30   Related to this radical idea is a second. This is the notion that illness, and the medical responses to illness, are intimately related to cultural worldviews. How we see the world structures how we experience and shape the world we live in. What makes particular responses seem reasonable emerges from
35   specific cultural values. The judgements about what medical practices are effective and sensible are value judgements made in the context of broader cultural beliefs about how the world works, our place in that world, and what is morally good and bad. Our aim is to help you understand why blood-letting, for
40   instance, now considered unacceptable, was a rational and sensible healing activity in the early 19th century.

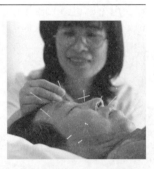

One of the great values of this approach is that it can help us better understand our own medical practice as intimately related to our cultural
45   worldview and better understand the unstated assumptions that guide it. Understanding that medical
50   practice has changed over time and is directly connected to cultural values gives us power to examine it in a new light. Nothing about our current practices is inevitable, and as citizens, we should feel empowered to demand that medicine be responsive to current human needs. 55

Finally, it is easy to read the history of medicine as one of constant progression, leading from barbaric roots to a sophisticated and universally correct scientific approach as embodied in current medical practice. We believe that this notion is problematic. First, a lack of knowledge that we have 60   today did not mean that medicine in other time periods and cultures was wrong. Based on cultural values and contemporary knowledge, other cultures developed advanced treatments that were effective and sensible for their people, although they may be considered barbaric nowadays. Similarly, in a century or two, 65   our own medical practices may seem backward and nonsensical. It is not the case that former practices have led simplistically to our own superior knowledge.

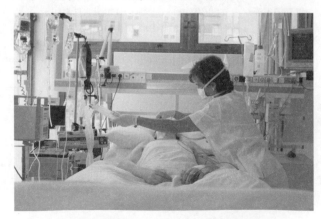

2 Answer these questions by choosing the correct letter, A, B, C or D. ⋯⋗ TF5

1 According to the first paragraph, the website is intended to show that
   A in the past, many illnesses were diagnosed wrongly.
   B medicine should be examined in connection with culture.
   C we have unrealistic expectations of medical practice.
   D changes in living conditions have led to the development of new illnesses.

2 What point is illustrated by the reference to fevers and chills (line 18)?
   A How an illness is interpreted affects how it is experienced.
   B Illnesses are influenced by climate and environment.
   C We need more accurate biological explanations of illnesses.
   D Our bodies are constantly under attack from illnesses.

3 What point is made in the third paragraph?
   A In certain cultures, the factual basis of illnesses is not recognised.
   B Medical practices have improved over time.
   C Illness can influence our perceptions of the world.
   D We judge past medical practices by inappropriate criteria.

4 What recommendation is made in the fourth paragraph?
   A We should be satisfied with current medical practice.
   B Medical practice should be explained to non-specialists.
   C We should value medicine more highly.
   D Medical practice should develop to meet our requirements.

5 What assumption is criticised in the last paragraph?
   A There are considerable differences between cultures.
   B Illnesses are better understood today than in the past.
   C Current medical practices will be seen differently in the future.
   D Too little research is being carried out into the treatment of certain diseases.

Vocabulary

3 For each verb and adjective, choose a noun to form the collocations that are used in the passage. Some other combinations are also possible.

Verbs	Nouns
1 to design	an illness
2 to feel	the world
3 to fight	pain
4 to practise	a website
5 to shape	a battle
6 to treat	medicine

Adjectives

7 cultural	approach
8 a historical	assumptions
9 a new	context
10 a scientific	judgements
11 unstated	light
12 value	values

4 These nouns and adjectives are used in this order in the reading passage. Beside each one, write the related verb.

1 experience ....
2 diagnosis ....
3 treatment ....
4 appreciation ....
5 relationship ....
6 practices ....
7 complementary ....
8 assumptions ....
9 responsive ....
10 progression ....

5 Complete these sentences with a noun formed from the verb in brackets.

1 Exposure to disease can give us lifetime (resist) .... to it.
2 It has been claimed that the (perceive) .... of illness changes over time.
3 Our approach to the treatment of illness is affected by the (assume) .... that we make about its nature.
4 I decided in (consult) .... with my doctor that I was fit enough to do a parachute jump.
5 Our (assess) .... of risk is not always based on rational criteria.
6 (fail) .... to evaluate risks rationally is often due to the amount of publicity that certain risks are given.

The human mind

Writing

1 Read this paragraph about personality, which is written in a fairly informal style.

Things happen to us because of our personality – chance doesn't have much to do with it. People who know about the brain and psychology think babies already have a personality. You can tell by what they do when things happen around them. The main things about our personality don't change much. By the time we're old enough to go to university, it's more or less fixed.

The following paragraph expresses similar ideas in a more academic style. Complete the paragraph by choosing the best words from the box, making any necessary changes to them.

act	establish	force	key	play	point
respond	suffer	undergo	wheel		

Our personality is the driving **1** .... behind the experiences we **2** .... , and the evidence suggests that chance may **3** .... only a small role. Some brain and psychological research strongly **4** .... to the fact that many of the **5** .... elements of our personality are present from birth, identifiable in the way our brain **6** .... to the world. Furthermore, they are firmly and largely irrevocably **7** .... by the time we are of university age.

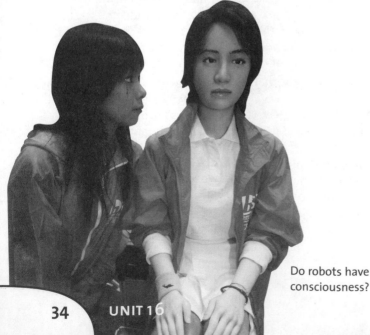

Do robots have consciousness?

Vocabulary

2 Match each of these definitions with the correct word in the box. This will help you when you read the passage on the opposite page, as all the words are used in it.

complementary	conscious	entity	equivalent
inference	investigate	pragmatic	soluble

1 awake, thinking and aware of what is happening around you
2 solving problems in a realistic way which suits the present conditions, rather than obeying fixed theories, ideas or rules
3 an opinion or guess that something is true based on the information that you have
4 capable of being solved (a problem)
5 having the same amount, value, purpose or qualities
6 to examine a crime, problem, statement, etc. carefully, especially to discover the truth
7 something which exists apart from other things, having its own independent existence
8 useful or attractive together, completing each other

Reading

3 Read the article on the opposite page, timing yourself as you read.

⏲ about 675 words

4 Look at the following theories and the list of people below. Match each theory with the person to whom it is ascribed. You may use any letter more than once. ⋯⟩ TF7

1 Consciousness may require certain materials to function in ways that we are unaware of.
2 Computers function because of the way they are organised, not the material they consist of.
3 The universe can be divided into consciousness and physical objects.
4 Science is limited to certain types of problems.
5 Computers may seem to think like human beings without actually doing so.
6 We can never be sure that other people are conscious.

List of People		
A Turing	**D** Penrose	**F** Descartes
B Searle	**E** Fenwick	**G** Berkeley
C Medawar		

What is consciousness?

Is the brain simply a computer, and is consciousness merely the feeling we get when we think? Or is consciousness a primary component of the universe, which the brain can tune in to, like a radio receiver?

There are three points of view. The first, which can be traced back to the founder of modern computing, Alan Turing, is pragmatic. Turing pointed out that it is impossible to know whether other human beings are conscious. Because we feel conscious, we assume other people must be like us. But this can only be an inference. However, suppose we made a computer – a robot – that could spontaneously behave like a person. It would appear conscious – and since, in judging the consciousness of others, appearances are all we have to go on, why not assume it is conscious?

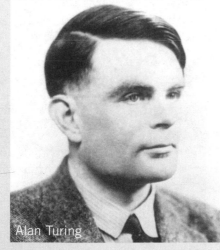
Alan Turing

This reasoning has the feel of the old saying: 'If it looks like a duck and quacks like a duck, then it is a duck' – adequate for some purposes, but of little use for understanding ducks and how they evolved. As the American philosopher John Searle has pointed out, it is possible to make computers that imitate all kinds of human thinking, but that does not mean they think as we do. An imitation of consciousness does not necessarily show consciousness.

Turing showed that a machine's ability to compute does not depend on what it is made of. All that matters is that the parts of the machine should be arranged appropriately. If a computer was sufficiently complex, then it, like the brain, would become conscious – or at least would appear to do so, which (so Turing said) is the only way to judge whether it is or not.

Searle's supporters ask us to imagine replacing a single neuron in the brain with a silicon chip that precisely imitates that neuron; that is, is 'functionally equivalent'. Would the brain still be conscious? The answer is surely 'yes'. If we continue to replace neurons, in the end we would have produced an all-silicon brain that retained the consciousness of the original.

However, we cannot replace even one of the billions of neurons in the brain with a 'functionally equivalent' microchip unless we understand the function of the original neuron. Yet complete understanding is impossible because, as the British zoologist Sir Peter Medawar commented, science is merely 'the art of the soluble'. Science answers only those questions that scientists ask and which they are technically able to investigate. It is impossible in theory, as well as in practice, to replace all the neurons of the brain with 'functionally equivalent' chips, since we can never know whether the replacement chips were functionally equivalent or not.

This leads on to a line of reasoning totally opposed to Turing's. Perhaps, some suggest, consciousness is not just a matter of computational complexity. Perhaps the material of which the brain is made matters very much, and only entities made of flesh are truly capable of consciousness.

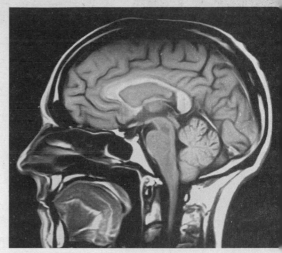

The Oxford mathematician Roger Penrose has suggested that consciousness involves physical principles not yet understood. Perhaps the flesh-and-blood brain has the chemistry required to use the physics required to produce consciousness, while silicon chips lack this ability?

An even more radical notion is being explored by physicists and brain specialists such as Dr Peter Fenwick. The idea is that philosophers and scientists have completely misunderstood the nature of consciousness and of the universe. For, until now, three main views have prevailed.

One is the 'dualism' of René Descartes (1596–1650), which says the universe has two components – matter (that is, physical substance or material) and mind. The second is the modern orthodox idea – that only matter 'exists'. The third, reflected in the philosophy of Bishop Berkeley (1685–1753), is that only thought is real, and matter is an illusion.

But the emerging modern view is that matter and consciousness are not separate entities, but *complementary* aspects of the universe, like two sides of a coin, or the space-time continuum. If this view of consciousness is right, our current understanding of science will be turned upside down.

Reading

1 Read this passage from an American magazine about the migration habits of the Monarch butterfly. Time yourself as you read.

⏱ about 500 words

The migration of the Monarch butterfly

It's fall in North America, and millions of Monarch butterflies are migrating to warmer climates for the winter, heading either to the Californian coast or to certain mountains in Mexico. These butterflies recognize the arrival of fall in the same way that we do: they feel the chill in the air. While we
5 adapt by putting on a sweater, the situation is much more serious for the Monarchs. Temperatures below 55°F make it impossible for them to take to the air; temperatures below 40°F paralyze them. The Monarchs originated in the tropics and can't live for long at temperatures below freezing.

At the same time that the air is cooling, the nectar supply in flowers that
10 feeds the butterflies is dwindling. To survive, they begin migrating in late summer, flying with the wind to reach their winter homes.

Up to 100 million Monarch butterflies migrate either to California or to Mexico each year. This isn't the entire population because some never make the migration. There are more than 25 winter roosting sites along the
15 Californian coast and about a dozen known sites in the Sierra Madre Oriental mountains of Mexico. In both regions, butterflies depend upon trees for their survival. They cluster in pine and eucalyptus trees along the California coast and in ovamel trees in Mexico.

Wintering Monarchs stay together. The end result looks like massive
20 clumps of feathery orange-and-black grapes. Each butterfly hangs with its wings over the butterfly beneath it, creating a shingle effect that buffers them from the rain and creates warmth. The weight of the cluster also prevents the butterflies from being blown away.

Butterflies stay in their winter homes until about March, when they
25 begin the return journey to their summer homes, travelling as fast as 30mph at times.

Monarch butterflies are in danger of losing both their summer and winter habitats. Summer habitats are being destroyed as more roads and new housing developments and business complexes encroach upon open
30 space in North America (a phenomenon known as urban sprawl).

As land is developed, the milkweed plant is killed. This is disastrous for the Monarch species, because once the butterfly larvae hatch from their eggs, they feed on this plant alone. Milkweed plants are also vulnerable to herbicides used by farmers, homeowners, landscapers, and gardeners.
35 The butterflies don't have it easy in Mexico, either. The ovamel trees that they winter in also serve as a lumber source for local communities and big logging companies. Logging not only removes the trees, it opens up the forest canopy as well, and in creating these overhead holes, the butterflies are potentially exposed to the life-threatening elements.
40 Each wintering site in Mexico contains millions of butterflies, and so damage to even one site could be a catastrophe for the Monarch butterfly population. Recent findings report that 44% of the ovamel forest has already been damaged or destroyed by logging.

2 **Do the following statements agree with the information in the passage?** ⋯▸ TF2
   For statements 1–10, choose

   TRUE   *if the statement agrees with the information*
   FALSE   *if the statement contradicts the information*
   NOT GIVEN   *if there is no information about this in the passage*

   1 The Monarch butterfly's ability to fly is affected by cool atmospheric conditions.
   2 The Monarch's migratory track changes according to wind direction.
   3 More Monarch butterflies migrate to California than to Mexico.
   4 Monarchs that spend the winter in California favour one type of tree.
   5 One reason why Monarchs collect in groups is to protect themselves from the wind.
   6 Because of climate change, Monarch butterflies now spend less time at winter locations than they used to.
   7 The Monarch can fly at a speed of more than 30 miles per hour.
   8 Construction work is putting the Monarch at risk.
   9 Monarch larvae depend on a single source of food.
   10 Man-made adjustments to the Mexican habitat have led to higher mortality rates.

Vocabulary

3 **Read the definitions and write the nouns in this word puzzle. They all come from the texts in this unit. The first letter for each one is given. What is the vertical word? Which other word in the puzzle does it relate to?**

   1 A calculation of the distance of a place from the equator
   2 Something that is observed to happen or exist
   3 The direction that someone or something is facing
   4 Movement from one place to another
   5 A piece of ground that is used for a particular purpose
   6 Another word for 'path'
   7 A small alteration or correction to something
   8 A visible feature which provides information about your location
   9 Unexpected oddities (plural form required)

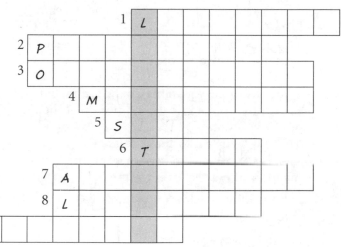

Writing

4 **Read part of an essay on the Irish Potato Famine below. Improve its academic style by rewriting it to include relative clauses and longer, more complex sentences.**

   The population of Ireland reached about 8.5 million by 1845. It had increased dramatically in the first half of the 19th century. Irish peasants depended on the potato as their single food crop. They favoured a variety called 'Aran Banner'. This potato was susceptible to a disease known as 'potato blight'. The disease had spread from North America to Europe.

   The Irish Potato Famine took hold in the winter of 1845–46. It was caused by a total crop failure. Irish towns and cities became ridden with diseases such as typhoid and cholera. Hundreds of thousands of starving people went for relief to the towns and cities. In 1848, there was a further outbreak of cholera. In 1848, the potato crop failed once again. Over 1.5 million people left Ireland in the late 1840s. They emigrated to Britain or North America.

   Start like this.

   The population of Ireland, which reached about 8.5 million by 1845, had increased dramatically in the first half of the 19th century.

Vocabulary

1 Add a negative prefix to each of these words. Check your answers in a dictionary.

EXAMPLE: plausible ....._implausible_.....

1 predictable ....
2 funded ....
3 informed ....
4 possible ....
5 practical ....
6 considered ....
7 valid ....

2 Use some of the words from exercise 1 to complete these sentences from the *Cambridge Academic Corpus*.

1 Some severely .... science departments have had to make savings in staff costs, which has in turn led to higher teaching loads.

2 This adds to the complexity of the argument, but does not, in my opinion, mean it is ....

3 Solutions to the equations can be found, but are so sensitive to the initial conditions that the outcome is very ....

4 Without further information, it is .... to deduce what the manuscript may have represented.

3 Match the idioms below to cartoons 1–3. One idiom isn't needed.

a have a hidden agenda
b cause a storm
c have a false ring
d be a can of worms

4 Complete these sentences with one of the idioms from exercise 3, adding any words in brackets.

EXAMPLE: Jack's explanation yesterday _had a very false ring_ (very) – I'm sure he's keeping something from me.

1 Dr Foot's assignment on modern poetry .... (real) – it's taking me much longer to complete than any of my other essays.

2 Dan Brown's novel .... (complete) and is selling out in bookshops everywhere.

3 Do you think that journalist .... ? Why is she asking for all this information now?

Grammar **G** ···▸ STUDENT'S BOOK page 143

Verbs followed by *wh-* clauses

5 Find 12 more verbs that can be followed by *wh-* clauses in this wordsearch (→↓).

S	D	I	S	C	O	V	E	R	N
P	E	S	T	I	M	A	T	E	E
E	S	A	O	C	R	R	R	S	V
C	C	S	H	O	W	E	E	S	A
U	R	S	C	N	R	F	A	I	L
L	I	E	S	S	E	L	L	H	U
A	B	S	U	I	M	E	I	R	A
T	E	S	U	D	I	C	S	L	T
E	X	E	R	E	N	T	E	E	E
P	L	A	N	R	D	O	U	B	T

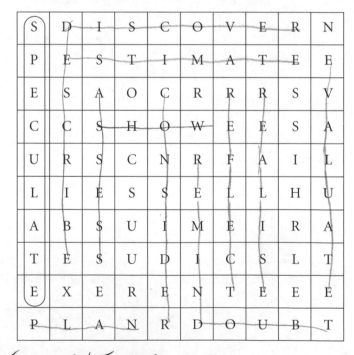

6 Complete this book review using some of the words from exercise 5 in a suitable tense or *-ing* form.

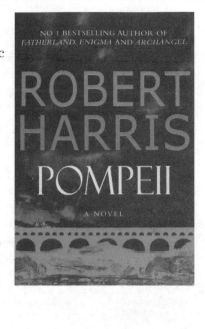

If you have ever **0** ....*speculated*........ how people behaved in the days leading up to the massive eruption of Vesuvius, then *Pompeii* by Robert Harris is the book for you. The novel takes place over four days, and specific time references at the beginning of each chapter **1** .... the reader what is inevitably going to happen. As the catastrophic event approaches, Harris vividly **2** .... what life was like for the Roman Empire's richest citizens in the late summer of AD 79, as they relaxed in their villas overlooking the Bay of Naples. The book is rich in historical detail, **3** .... how carefully Harris did his research. At the same time, Harris has produced a superb thriller. I **4** .... whether a more gripping account has ever been written on Pompeii. The hero of the novel, engineer Marcus Attilius, has to **5** .... why the fresh water supply to the quarter of a million people living around the Bay of Naples is failing. As he struggles to **6** .... whether the 60-mile aqueduct is still functioning, he soon **7** .... what an enormous task he has undertaken. Attilius remains optimistic, and, being a practical man, he immediately **8** .... how to repair the aqueduct and restore the water supply. However, as the reader knows only too well, the forces of nature will eventually overpower him and devastate an entire area.

7 Complete the second sentences with the verb in brackets and a *wh-* word, including any pronouns necessary.

EXAMPLE: 'The reason for the delay on my essay is that I have been ill,' said Carla. (explain)

Carla *is explaining why her* essay is late.

1 'There were probably around 65 students attending yesterday's lecture,' said Dr Rogers. (estimate)
Dr Rogers .... the attendance of yesterday's lecture was.

2 'If I were you, I'd accept the offer from Bristol University,' said John's tutor. (advise)
John's tutor .... university to choose.

3 'Shall we go to Spain next week or stay at home?' said Ken. (ask)
Ken .... they should go to Spain or not.

4 'I haven't been able to get any information on Michel Butor,' said Maya. (find out)
Maya .... Michel Butor is.

5 'Why not chop the onions and fry them quickly in a little olive oil?' said Jamie. (suggest)
Jamie .... to cook the onions.

6 'I know you think the lab results are OK, but I'm less convinced,' said Dr Forrester. (question)
Dr Forrester .... the lab results are acceptable.

Earning a living

Reading

1 Read the article below, which is a short version of something you might find in the General Training Reading Module. Time yourself as you read. As you read, choose the correct heading for each paragraph from the list of headings below. This task is used in both Reading Modules. ⋯⫶ TF1

List of Headings

i	A balance can be negotiated to suit individual needs
ii	There are advantages for both sides
iii	Someone else has to do part of your job
iv	The benefits are sometimes unexpected
v	A broader range of employees can benefit
vi	The requirements of both employers and staff have changed
vii	Some workers may be disappointed
viii	Work can take over your life

1 Paragraph A
2 Paragraph B
3 Paragraph C
4 Paragraph D
5 Paragraph E

⏱ about 450 words

Finding a work/life balance

A Like many people in full-time employment, you may be experiencing increasing pressure to stay late at night, take work home or just 'pop into the office' at the weekend. As a result, you may feel growing dissatisfaction, as you find the boundaries between life and work beginning to blur, and all your enthusiasm and energy getting used up on the job. On the other hand, finding your job satisfying does not make you want to spend all your time at work either, as other things in your life matter, too. The good news is that some employers are making it easier to find a balance.

B One firm which does is the engineering company that Andre Geelan works for. Canoe polo isn't a high-profile sport, but Andre has spent years working very hard at it, and represents his state in the Australian national championships. He's also an engineer who spends a lot of work time offshore on oil rigs. Before the national titles, Andre trains three nights a week and most of Saturdays. 'It can be a bit of a problem with work because I often get sent offshore at very short notice and can be away for days,' he says. However, Andre discusses his canoe-polo commitments with his line manager, who does his best to build them into the work schedule. Geelan is finding it easier to arrange time off when he wants it as he becomes more experienced in the job – and more important to his employer.

C The workplace in Australia, as in many other countries, is significantly different from what it was not all that long ago. It needs a more flexible, skilled and responsive workforce. At the same time, employees are increasingly looking for flexible working conditions which acknowledge lifestyle choices, including family, self-education, progressive return to the workplace or easing out of the workforce altogether.

D The term 'work/life balance' has gained wide currency, as employers recognise that their staff may have a life outside the office. When it works, it's a win-win situation. The employee has greater flexibility, and the employer is rewarded with greater commitment, higher staff morale and reduced absenteeism.

E Work/life balance developed out of the 'family-friendly' policies introduced in the late 80s and early 90s. Where family-friendly polices were mainly seen as a women's initiative, designed to support mothers with children, work/life balance is less gender specific and recognises other commitments as well as family. A number of policies and practices, such as flexible working hours, working from home and job sharing, make an organisation more responsive to the needs of its workforce. So if you're looking to improve your work/life balance, try talking to your boss.

2 Complete the summary below using words from the box.

> accommodate   benefit   enjoy   follow
> increase   negotiate   reconsider   refuse
> require   reward   suffer   train

Both employees who are under pressure and those who **1** .... their jobs may begin to **2** .... their work/life balance. Some, like Andre Geelan, are satisfied: he needs time to **3** .... , and his employer is willing to **4** .... his sporting commitments. The demands of a variety of situations may mean that employees **5** .... flexibility at work. Organisations that provide it are likely to **6** .... , as it may well influence the attitudes of staff towards their work.

Vocabulary

3 Complete these sentences using words related to those in the box. All the words were used on page 125 of the Student's Book.

> applicants   appointments   catering
> customers   expenses   experience   profit
> property   qualifications   refurbishment
> ~~staff~~   suppliers

1 At first, the Hendersons worked long hours themselves, because they couldn't afford the ....*staffing*......... levels that they wanted.

2 The restaurant .... for people who want inexpensive meals and don't want to book.

3 An average of ten people .... for each vacancy.

4 The Hendersons decided to .... chefs who had already worked in restaurants for a few years.

5 Daniel .... as an accountant several years before opening the restaurant.

6 The property was in poor condition, so it had to be .... quite extensively.

7 As they became more .... , running the restaurant became easier.

8 They've found a very good small business that now .... them with fresh fish.

9 When the restaurant becomes more .... , the Hendersons will consider opening a new one.

4 Read this paragraph quickly, then complete the paraphrase below with words related to ones in the paragraph. The first one is given. Write NO MORE THAN ONE WORD for each answer.

> **Work is a burden for those in their 30s**
> A new study of workers in their 30s has found that many long to leave the jobs they are currently doing. More and more employees perceive that the traditional model of being promoted from one job to another is unsuitable for them. Increasingly, they expect to be satisfied with their job, but are disappointed, so consider doing something else. The researchers found that many people strongly desire to reduce the number of hours they work or become self-employed. Most, however, are too anxious to make the move, because they are focusing on saving for when they retire. The minority who start their own businesses generally feel more fulfilled.

A new study of workers in their 30s has identified a **1** ......*longing*...... to leave their **2** .... jobs. There is a growing **3** .... that the traditional model of **4** .... is unsuitable. Increasingly, their **5** .... of job satisfaction lead to **6** .... , so they consider alternatives. The researchers found a strong **7** .... for a **8** .... in working hours, or the opportunity to become self-employed. Most, however, are held back from making the move by **9** .... , because they are focusing on saving for their **10** .... The minority who start their own businesses generally find greater **11** ....

Well, that's enough work for today.
Time I went home and relaxed.

It's history

Reading

1 **Read this introduction to a book about clothing fashions. Time yourself as you read.**

⏱ about 650 words

Fashion in European costume

A Our inventiveness in manipulating a length of cloth into a three-dimensional shape to cover the human body has been demonstrated with astonishing variety over the past few centuries. The continuous desire for change in dress cannot be dismissed as arbitrary. Fashion, whether in art, architecture, furniture or dress, must rather be seen as the expression of ideas shared by a number of people at any one time, often linked to fundamental changes in moral or social values, and thus reflecting the essential characteristics of a particular period; and dress should be regarded as an art form, a skilful arrangement of materials through which ideas or messages, both personal and social, are communicated.

B Articles of clothing were first used in this way as symbols of rank, authority or occupation, a function that still survives in, for instance, a king's crown, a bishop's mitre and cope, special robes for judges and the whole range of uniforms for military or specialised services. From these specific symbols developed the use of clothes to convey less obvious or direct messages, such as the superiority of one individual over another, particularly in terms of wealth (which frequently also meant power), indicated by jewels, rich fabrics and furs, or garments in which it would be difficult to undertake physical labour. Even today, the desire to wear a mink coat, diamonds or ostentatious clothing as a sign of financial and social success is not uncommon.

C The need to achieve status and win admiration is a fundamental human instinct, however subconscious, and is reflected in our choice of clothing. Few people are completely indifferent to the clothes they wear; even those who choose to dress 'out of fashion' in what they consider a more aesthetic manner and those who are negligent or even slovenly often achieve a sense of superiority in being unconventional. But there is also a strong urge to belong; we are social animals and need to feel at one with the community. Fashion in clothing is therefore an expression of the communal ideas or beliefs of a social group, and changes in society often lead to new styles. There were significant changes in fashion when women gained greater freedom during the 1920s, and again in the 1960s, with the glorification of youth and the revolt against the status quo.

D The desire to be admired for physical beauty also plays an important part in costume. In seeking to achieve the ideal fashionable image, dress has been used to accentuate good points and disguise shortcomings. Success in attracting the opposite sex has been consistently admired and envied, but physical ideals have varied widely, noticeably rather more so for women than men during the 19th and 20th centuries.

E Why should men and women dress differently? The assumption since the mid-16th century that skirts are correct for women and not for men was fairly obviously brought about by roles they were called upon to play in society, underlined by religious pressures. Women dressed in garments that hampered their movements, and it may be that such garments were originally an indication of a lady's privileged position. However, most upper- and middle-class women, forced until comparatively recently to accept marriage as the only respectable career, had for practical reasons to look for social advancement or financial stability in a husband if they had any choice at all, while men, who had greater freedom, might be attracted into marriage by beauty alone; and this may have encouraged what has been referred to as the seduction principle in women's dress, with a constant change of emphasis on different parts of the anatomy to stimulate interest and attention. With less religious pressure and greater equality between the sexes in the last few decades, men and women have often worn similar clothes.

2 The reading passage has five paragraphs labelled A–E. Which paragraph contains the following information? You may use any letter more than once. ⋯⟿ TF8

1 reasons for some resemblance between men's and women's clothing
2 examples of clothes assigned to particular areas of responsibility
3 a claim concerning the use of clothing to hide limitations in one's appearance
4 what clothing may have in common with other fields
5 the possible role of clothing in feeling that one is a member of a social group
6 why women used to need to dress in a way that appealed to men
7 a suggestion concerning the motivation of people who go against fashion

3 Complete the summary below using words from the box. Remember that the summary must reflect the meaning of the passage. ⋯⟿ TF 10

admirable	affluent	creative	formal
manual	planned	prevailing	random
rebellious	symbolic		

Clothes design shows how **1** .... people have been over the centuries. Changes in fashion do not seem to be **2** .... , but instead they mirror changes in the **3** .... ideas of a society. Clothing can be informative about both individuals and whole societies, initially indicating established positions in society. Subsequently, people showed how **4** .... they were, for instance by wearing clothes unsuitable for **5** .... work.
Fashions in clothing have changed, for example to reflect the **6** .... mood of the 1960s.

4 Complete this summary. Choose NO MORE THAN ONE WORD from the passage for each answer.

Until recently, men and women dressed differently because of their different **1** ....
Women's clothes showed their **2** .... social status, compared with men; also, with **3** .... as their only acceptable course of action, clothing was a way of drawing **4** .... to women's beauty. Nowadays, men's and women's clothes are less distinct, because of increasing **5** ....

Grammar G ⋯⟿ STUDENT'S BOOK page 143

Modal perfects

5 Choose the correct modal form in each of these sentences.

1 If the social changes of the 1920s hadn't occurred, fashions in women's clothing *should / would* probably have been very different.
2 The French revolution in the late 18th century *may / must* possibly have led to a change in fashions in clothing.
3 Middle-class women's clothing in the 19th century was so restrictive that it *can't / mustn't* have been very comfortable.
4 I *couldn't / shouldn't* have followed the advice my lawyer gave me – it caused more problems than it solved.
5 I *couldn't / wouldn't* have bought these shoes if I'd realised they would be so tight.
6 The writer's arguments are hard to follow – they *could / may* have been expressed more clearly.
7 Nineteenth-century dress designers *must / shouldn't* have known that many of their creations would be very uncomfortable.
8 I enjoyed my trip round the world so much that I *should / would* have done it years ago.
9 Thank you very much for this necklace. I *can't / couldn't* have asked for a better present.
10 If women had had more freedom to choose their clothes, they *can't / may not* have worn what they did.

Vocabulary

6 For each word below, choose two synonyms from the box. Many of the words were used in Unit 20 of the Student's Book.

ambition	comprehension	distortion
dream	follow	forestall	impartial
misconception	misrepresentation	mistake
outcome	prevent	replace	result
unbiased	understanding	

1 aspiration .... , ...
2 avert .... , ...
3 consequence .... , ...
4 falsification .... , ...
5 illusion .... , ...
6 objective (adj.) .... , ...
7 perception .... , ...
8 succeed .... , ...

Writing workout 1: Structuring an essay

Academic Writing Task 2

1 Decide which parts of the advice below on essay writing are helpful. Write 'Y' if you agree with the statement and 'N' if you disagree.

1 Make a plan to organise your ideas before you start writing.
2 Check that all your ideas are relevant to the topic.
3 Repeat the actual words from the question wherever possible.
4 Include an introduction that indicates your views on the topic.
5 Use only minimal paragraphing.
6 Make extensive use of rhetorical questions.
7 Restate your overall opinion in a conclusion.
8 Leave enough time to check spelling and grammar.

2 Read this task and tick all the sentences (A–J) that seem relevant to the topic.

> Write about the following topic.
>
> ***In today's world, the dominance of global product brands is increasingly threatening our identity as individuals.***
>
> ***How far do you agree or disagree with this statement?***
>
> Give reasons for your answer and include any relevant examples from your own knowledge or experience.
>
> Write at least 250 words.

A At the same time, not every branded product carries the same importance when it comes to a declaration of lifestyle.
B Most supermarkets sell their own brand of products alongside those made by other companies.
C Even the most globally available products have to be advertised differently in different parts of the world.
D Some individuals in the world of entertainment function like brand names.
E The favouring of global brands is sometimes itself a reaction against tradition and upbringing.
F Sometimes people choose a certain brand because they associate it with positive images of life.
G Brand names appear to be largely irrelevant when it comes to everyday products.
H Take Coca-Cola, for example, which is sold virtually everywhere.
I People become 'de-personalised' in an institution such as a prison.
J It erases cultural differences and makes the world less interesting as a result.

3 Now read this sample answer. Think about possible missing content in the numbered spaces and then choose suitable sentences from those in exercise 2.

It is true that some branded products can be bought all over the world. 1 .... Does its popularity as a soft drink mean that we are losing our identity? Considered on its own, probably not, but the combination of many branded products may indeed have some impact on our way of life.

2 .... For instance, others may make assumptions about who you are according to the type of car you drive, but they will be far less likely to judge you on the basis of which toilet paper you buy. 3 ....

In addition, although many international brands are becoming more and more widespread, they still have to conform to local conditions and expectations. 4 .... This clearly proves that our identity is 'alive and well', rather than being under threat.

Is 'identity' only defined by what we buy? Surely there are other influences shaping us as individuals, such as parents and teachers. 5 .... This undermining of local values is perhaps a more crucial issue than that of the individual. 6 ....

4 Rewrite the following pairs of sentences as one sentence, using the word or phrase in brackets and making any other changes needed.

1 Companies are investing in international sales and marketing campaigns. Some brands are now available globally. (because)

....
....
....

2 Coca-Cola is popular everywhere. Many local soft drinks are popular, too. (although)

....
....
....

3 International brands may not sell worldwide. International brands are marketed competently. (unless)

....
....
....
....

4 International products are advertised locally. Adverts for international brands must conform to local expectations. (when)

....
....
....
....

5 Identity is partly defined by what we buy. Identity is also influenced by our relationships. (if)

....
....
....
....

5 Choose the best underlined alternative to complete this introduction to the answer in exercise 3.

1 *Although / Unless* it is true that 2 *noticeably / extremely* well-known international brands are becoming more readily available, there is little evidence that they 3 *should / could* destroy a person's identity, 4 *according to me / in my opinion*. The reasons for this are 5 *sketched / outlined* below.

6 Correct the ten spelling errors in this conclusion to the answer in exercise 3.

To conclud, it is definitly the case that global brands are increaseingly present in the lifes of many peopel around the world, but they do not neccessarily threaten a person's identity. Personaly, what I find of greater concern is the likly affect on local cultur and customs.

7 Read this task and make notes of your ideas using the paragraph plan.

> Write about the following topic.
>
> **Email and text messaging have transformed communication, but they are seriously threatening the status of written language.**
>
> **How far do you agree or disagree with this statement?**
>
> Give reasons for your answer and include any relevant examples from your own knowledge or experience.
>
> Write at least 250 words.

Paragraph plan

- Introduction

....
....
....
....

- Communication methods before the invention of email and mobile phones

....
....
....
....

- Benefits of email and text messaging

....
....
....
....

- Possible threats to written language

....
....
....
....

- Conclusion

....
....
....
....

Writing workout 2: Developing language range

Academic Writing Tasks 1 and 2

1 Complete this paragraph, using one word only in each space.

For **0** ......*both*...... tasks in the Academic Writing Module, it is important to use as wide a variety of language **1** .... possible. By doing **2** .... , you will be able **3** .... give the examiner a better idea **4** .... your language range. This means using different structures – such **5** .... conditionals, adverbial clauses and passive forms – and a lot of different vocabulary. **6** .... particular, good use of a variety of adjectives and adverbs will demonstrate your vocabulary range. It may **7** .... matter if you spell some of these words inaccurately, since what matters above **8** .... is that you are showing your knowledge of different words.

2 Form an adjective or adverb related to the word in brackets to complete each sentence.

1 There are many new gadgets available for those of us who are more (technology) .... minded.

2 It is (meaning) .... to label plastics as being dangerous to our health without quantifying any actual risks.

3 The singer is very (manipulation) .... and always manages to upset the performers who have to work with him.

4 (real) .... , man will not explore beyond the solar system within our lifetime.

5 Many scientists regret the fact that they have not developed their (artist) .... side to any extent.

6 All the members of the band behave very (prediction) .... during live concerts, and their manager often has to apologise for the damage caused.

7 Plastics are now being used most (effect) .... in the manufacturing of new fashion fabrics.

8 (finance) .... speaking, the restaurant is struggling to survive, but it has had some excellent reviews recently.

3 Read the task and sample answer, ignoring the spaces for the moment. Does the writer agree or disagree with the statement?

> Write about the following topic.
>
> *Due to the success of convenience food and ready-made meals, we are failing to pass on adequate culinary skills to the next generation.*
>
> *To what extent do you agree or disagree with this statement?*
>
> Give reasons for your answer and include any relevant examples from your own knowledge or experience.
>
> Write at least 250 words.

In today's **1** .... β world, where both parents are usually working full time, the **2** .... dependence on ready-made meals should come as no surprise. Even people without children show little desire to cook a **3** .... meal after working all day, which is entirely **4** .... If they are earning and can afford to buy convenience food or go out to restaurants, why shouldn't they? At the same time, it cannot be denied that because of this, we are losing the ability to cook **5** .... meals at home.

The fact is that ready-made meals are not usually that good for us. They contain high levels of salt and sugar, not to mention **6** .... preservatives and artificial colorants. A diet that is exclusively made up of such food is bound to be unhealthy.

Moreover, it is extremely important for children to learn how to cook, so that they will be fully **7** .... when they grow up. Given that schools have no time to devote to cooking on the curriculum, the only place where children can learn **8** .... culinary skills is in the home.

Speaking personally, I have always enjoyed experimenting in the kitchen, by cooking slightly **9** .... meals. Whatever recipe I decide on, I only use **10** .... seasonal ingredients. Both my mother and father cook at home, and I have learned a lot of useful tips from them. If I have children of my own, I shall make sure that they learn how to cook as soon as they are old enough to enjoy the experience.

In conclusion, although some use of convenience food is natural, no one should rely on it exclusively at the expense of home-cooked food. Not only is this unhealthy but it is also threatening important skills with extinction.

4　Choose the best adjective, A, B or C, to fill spaces 1–10 in the answer in exercise 3. Where more than one adjective is possible, choose the less common one. Use a dictionary to check meaning if necessary.

1	**A** slaving	**B** stressful	**C** unrelaxing
2	**A** advanced	**B** multiplied	**C** increased
3	**A** complicated	**B** difficult	**C** problematic
4	**A** sympathetic	**B** intelligible	**C** understandable
5	**A** nutritious	**B** supportive	**C** good
6	**A** bad	**B** harmful	**C** deadly
7	**A** alone	**B** single	**C** independent
8	**A** basic	**B** top	**C** main
9	**A** improbable	**B** disorderly	**C** unconventional
10	**A** pure	**B** fresh	**C** new

5　Use passive forms of the verbs in brackets to complete this rewritten conclusion to the answer in exercise 3.

In conclusion, although it is natural for some use
1 (make) .... of convenience food, it 2 (rely) .... on
exclusively at the expense of food 3 (prepare) .... at home.
Not only is this unhealthy but also means that important skills
4 (threaten) .... with extinction.

6　Look at the illustrations below. They show a simple recipe for twice-baked potatoes. Write a description of the process based on the pictures, using a range of passive forms of the verbs in the box. Start as shown below.

| bake | combine | cut | leave | mash | place | put |
| remove | return | rub | scoop | stuff | | |

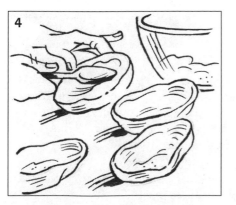

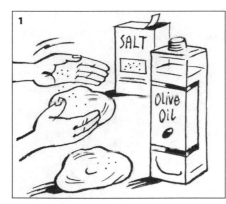

Large potatoes should be chosen for this recipe. Having been
washed and dried, each potato ...

Writing workout 3: Comparing and contrasting

Academic Writing Task 1

1 Decide which parts of the advice below on Task 1 are helpful. Write 'Y' if you agree with the statement and 'N' if you disagree.

  1 Spend no more than 20 minutes on the task.
  2 Try to write around 180 words.
  3 Focus on the main trends shown.
  4 Don't waste words on an introduction.
  5 Use comparative structures with qualifiers where appropriate.
  6 Include as many figures as possible.

2 Sort the jumbled letters and write the qualifiers in the spaces provided, starting with the letter in bold.

  1 h **o** s t m w e a ....
  2 x l a t e c y ....
  3 n t i e y r e l ....
  4 a r e t h **r** ....

3 Look at the graphic information below, showing current and projected energy consumption and carbon dioxide (CO_2) emissions for the USA and China. Decide whether sentences 1–8 are true or false.

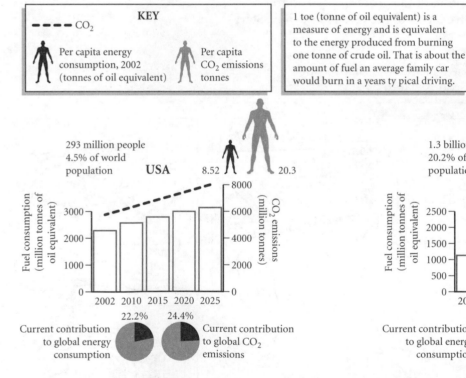

KEY

- - - - CO_2

Per capita energy consumption, 2002 (tonnes of oil equivalent)

Per capita CO_2 emissions tonnes

1 toe (tonne of oil equivalent) is a measure of energy and is equivalent to the energy produced from burning one tonne of crude oil. That is about the amount of fuel an average family car would burn in a years typical driving.

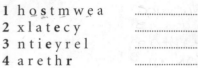

293 million people
4.5% of world population

USA 8.52 20.3

1.3 billion people
20.2% of world population

China 0.88 2.7

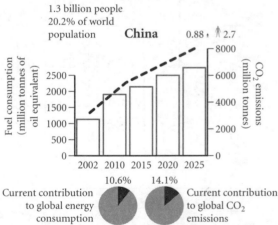

22.2% 24.4%

Current contribution to global energy consumption

Current contribution to global CO_2 emissions

10.6% 14.1%

Current contribution to global energy consumption

Current contribution to global CO_2 emissions

1 Considering the current size of each population, average fuel consumption in the USA is substantially higher than that of China.

2 In 2002, China consumed approximately half the amount of fuel that was consumed by the USA.

3 The USA currently accounts for just under 25% of global carbon-dioxide emissions, while China contributes around 14%.

4 By 2020, it is likely that the USA and China will be consuming virtually the same amount of fuel.

5 Fuel consumption in the USA is predicted to rise by 2025 to around 3,000 million toes (tonnes of oil equivalent), whereas consumption in China by 2025 will be just over 2,500 toes.

6 Carbon-dioxide emissions in the USA are forecast to rise steadily to 2025.

7 Carbon-dioxide emissions in China are projected to rise sharply until 2015, when they will level off.

8 In 2002, the level of carbon-dioxide emissions in China was less than half that of the USA.

4   Complete the text below, which relates to the graphic information on Japan
    and India, by writing one word only or a number in each space.

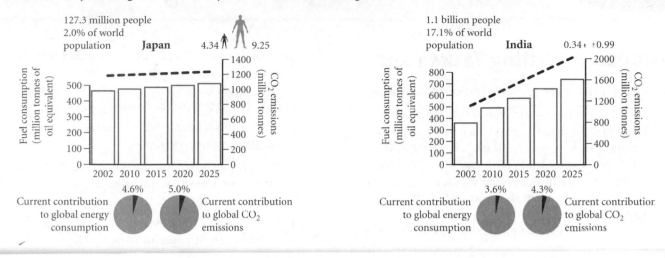

The **1** .... charts illustrate fuel consumption and the **2** .... graphs plot carbon-dioxide emissions. From the accompanying pie charts, it can be seen that Japan currently uses 4.6% of the world's energy. However, only **3** .... for 2% of the world's population, this is considerably **4** .... per capita than India, which contributes 3.6% of global energy consumption, but has a population of 1.1 billion people, just **5** .... 17% of the global total.

Japan's fuel consumption in 2002 was significantly higher than India's, but India is projected to overtake Japan in this respect by **6** .... Japan's predicted increase in energy use is relatively slight over the period, while India's is set to **7** .... by 2025.

Although India's level of carbon-dioxide emissions in 2002 was slightly **8** .... than Japan's (circa 1,100 million tonnes as **9** .... to around 1,200 million tonnes), India's emissions are forecast to rise sharply to 2025, whereas Japan's will probably **10** .... off.

5   Now answer the task below, which contains similar information for South Korea and Australia.

> You should spend about 20 minutes on this task.
>
> **The charts and illustrations below show current and projected energy consumption and carbon-dioxide emissions for South Korea and Australia.**
>
> **Summarise the information by selecting and reporting the main features, and make comparisons where relevant.**
>
> Write at least 150 words.

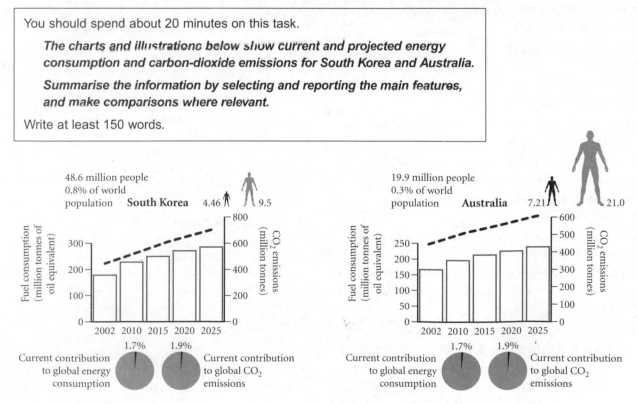

Writing workout 4: Checking for accuracy

Academic Writing Tasks 1 and 2

1 Correct the spelling errors in the advice below.

In the Academic Writting Module, you only have an hour to complete the two tasks. Make sure you leave enought time to give yourself the oportunity to check both your answers thoroghly. Make any corections neatly and legibley. Errors often occur when a letter is silent, for example in the words *goverment*, *tecnology* and *othewise*. Be especialy carefull with vowel combinations in words such as *beautiful* and *enourmous*. Also, remember to check that you have added any suffixes accurately: *-ness* and *-ful* are often misspelled.

2 Read this task. Then read sentences A–J and correct any errors in word order. Write the corrected sentences in the appropriate part of the paragraph plan.

> Write about the following topic.
>
> **People face far greater risks in our modern way of life than they did in the past.**
>
> **How far do you agree or disagree with this statement?**
>
> Give reasons for your answer and include any relevant examples from your own knowledge or experience.
>
> Write at least 250 words.

A People used to have rarely as long a life expectancy as we enjoy today.

B The streets of our cities are probably now safer to walk in than they were a hundred years ago.

C Modern inventions like nuclear power plants could be perceived as life-threatening, although in reality, a dangerous incident is extremely unlikely to occur.

D It is true that people choose sometimes in their choice of leisure activities to take risks.

E We are undoubtedly today at risk of injury from the cars we drive, a threat that in the past was absent.

F Thanks to advances in modern medicine, we are protected better from deadly diseases nowadays.

G Natural disasters such as earthquakes have been always a part of life, though it could be argued that we are now facing disasters on a larger scale, due to severe weather trends.

H We have to consider what are the causes of this obesity and heart disease.

I In fact, we are far more likely in the home to injure ourselves than outside, which has probably always been the case.

J Newspapers and television are partly responsible for the current perception of risk from violent attacks.

Paragraph plan

● Health and illness

....
....
....
....
....
....

● Personal risk-taking and accidents

....
....
....
....
....
....

● Crime

....
....
....
....
....

● Catastrophic events

....
....
....
....
....

3 A recurrent area of grammar error for IELTS candidates is in tenses. Read the relevant Grammar folder section in the Student's Book for more information. Then correct the sentences below.

- past simple/present perfect **G**⋯⟩ p 138
- past simple or present perfect / past perfect **G**⋯⟩ p 138
- tenses in conditional structures **G**⋯⟩ p 139
- present simple or future simple **G**⋯⟩ p 141

1 One year later, the company send me on a merchandising training session.
2 In my essay, I am discussing the merits and demerits of the mobile phone.
3 I am glad to welcome you and your family next week.
4 Our parents have respected their teachers more than we do.
5 It is a pity that there are so many students who have enrolled in the university but lived with their family.
6 Before computers, if you want to write something, you had to write it with a pen or pencil.
7 I've now been to some of the places I've been dreaming of as a child.
8 Last week, they hold a family meeting where they decided they will watch TV for only three hours a day.
9 Parents feel that if their child will become an artist, it will be difficult for him or her financially.
10 Nowadays man was influenced by scientific inventions.

4 Here are some errors made by IELTS candidates. Replace the word which has been used wrongly with the correct word, chosen from the box above the sentences. There is one extra word in each box.

available	lowest	modern	poor
popular	prompt		

1 The least percentage of tourists was ten.
2 Your earlier action will be appreciated.
3 Nevertheless, her general condition is still fair and requires special care.
4 The least preferable activities were hobbies.
5 Computers have a vast number of uses in the present world.

drawbacks	effects	events	facilities
goods	hours	methods	negotiations
numbers	scenes	values	

6 The chart shows the amount spent on six consumer goals in four European countries.
7 I work in an organisation where the office timings are from nine to six.
8 Some pictures in films are unsuitable for children.
9 Our country has received a lot of aid to help maintain our infrastructure, health institutes and agricultural schemes.
10 They depended on old ways of communication like drum-beating and lighting fires.
11 Children should be taught that they have responsibility for the efforts of their actions.
12 I've also been in charge of price dealings with our partners.
13 There is a proposal to hold art parties in public places.
14 The benefits of computers are greater than the losses.
15 In 1980, the amounts of scientists and technicians in developing countries was three times smaller than in industrialised countries.

5 Add your ideas to the paragraph plan in exercise 2. Then answer the task in at least 250 words.

Writing workout 5: Using appropriate language

Academic Writing Tasks 1 and 2

1 Tick the features you consider appropriate to academic writing from this list.

1 Neutral/formal language ☐
2 Impersonal style ☐
3 Cautious tone ☐
4 Colloquial language ☐
5 Non-aggressive tone ☐
6 Informal language ☐
7 Serious tone ☐
8 Humorous style ☐

2 Choose the best alternatives in italics in these sentences to soften the tone (1–6) or make the style more impersonal (7–10).

1 The statement is *rather* / *highly* flawed because it *suggests* / *argues* that one element rules out the other.
2 This claim makes *no* / *little* sense, especially when read out of context.
3 It is *really* / *somewhat* illogical to compare these two aspects, given that they are *wildly* / *so* different.
4 *Perhaps* / *Unquestionably* the first question that *must* / *should* be asked is what is implied by such a statement.
5 In fact, there are *a number of* / *hundreds of* reasons which could be given to refute such a claim.
6 It is *a little* / *very* hard to understand what is actually meant here.
7 In any case, *I reckon that* / *it is likely that* job security is a thing of the past.
8 *You cannot deny* / *It cannot be denied* that both aspects are desirable, in an ideal world.
9 First and foremost, what *is meant* / *does the writer mean* by this term?
10 *I totally agree with him that* / *It is absolutely right to suggest, as the writer does, that* there is only a tenuous link between the two aspects.

3 Match the informal words (1–7) with their neutral or formal equivalent (a–g).

1 folks   a line manager
2 cash   b difficult
3 boring   c tedious
4 crazy   d meaningless
5 tough   e funds
6 boss   f people
7 silly   g irrational

4 Replace the phrasal verbs used in this paragraph with more formal equivalents chosen from the box, in the correct form. One verb is not needed.

behave	complain	display	exploit
labour	pause	spend	

Many people **1** *slave away* .... in the same mundane job for years, without ever once **2** *sounding off* .... to their employers. They never **3** *break off* .... for a moment to consider whether they are being **4** *ripped off* .... because, for them, security is what counts. For this reason, they **5** *knuckle under* .... and make the best of things. Considering that so many of our waking hours are **6** *dragged out* .... in the workplace, this is a rather dismal state of affairs.

5 Read this task and the sample answer on the next page. Rewrite the underlined parts using some of the language in exercises 3 and 4, or your own words, to improve the style and tone of the answer.

Write about the following topic.

> *Job satisfaction is far less important than job security in the modern workplace.*
>
> *How far do you agree or disagree with this statement?*

Give reasons for your answer and include any relevant examples from your own knowledge or experience.

Write at least 250 words.

It appears ——

<u>I reckon</u> the statement is a little flawed, because even in today's uncertain times, <u>you can</u> still find both satisfaction and security in many areas of current employment. Moreover, it is <u>crazy</u> to suggest that one aspect is more important than the other, given that they are <u>like chalk and cheese</u>. It is a rather <u>silly</u> generalisation to <u>come up with</u>, in any case.

It goes without saying that, for some individuals, long-term job prospects are <u>100% important</u>, perhaps because they are <u>forking out</u> considerable sums of money each month and need to be confident in their ongoing ability to find <u>the cash</u>. On the other hand, for <u>other folks</u> who have fewer personal commitments or are generally more flexible, security will be less of <u>a thing</u>.

<u>And another thing</u>, job satisfaction is something that is rather <u>tough</u> to measure. It cannot be denied that <u>most of us</u> would prefer to do a job that is rewarding, rather than have to <u>slog away</u> at a job that is <u>utterly boring</u>. However, there are many ways to measure job satisfaction. It may be a personal reaction to success or impact in the job, that is to say, <u>the chances of getting things done</u>. Or it may stem from the working atmosphere: working for an inspirational <u>boss</u>, for example, or with colleagues who are worthy of respect.

In the final analysis, individual circumstances will influence a person's ability to find the job that is right for them, and will also dictate whether they try to <u>hang on to</u> it in the long term.

Reading module

Advice on tackling the Reading Module

The Reading Module as a whole

- Spend **60 minutes** on the Reading Module, without any breaks.
- Spend no more than **20 minutes** on each passage. If you spend longer on the first one or two, you won't be able to finish the third.
- You must write your answers on the **Answer Sheet** (see page 64). There is no extra time for doing this. You can write on the Question Paper, but make sure you copy your answers accurately onto the Answer Sheet within the 60 minutes.
- Remember that each question gives you **one mark**, so don't spend a long time on a single question.
- As far as possible, give an **answer to every question**.
- Remember that **you don't need to understand every word**.

Each Reading Passage

- If there is a headings task, it will appear *before* the passage. Read it quickly before reading the passage.
- Read the **title** and spend about **two to three minutes skimming** the passage. **Mark important information**, such as the main point in each paragraph (often in the first sentence of the paragraph). This will help you to find the relevant part of the passage for each task and question. Ignore details.
- **Don't worry** if you find the passage difficult to understand. You'll probably understand more of it when you try to answer the questions.
- Look at the first task. Read the **instructions** (rubric) carefully and **underline important information**, such as the maximum number of words to give. Advice on each task type is given in the Test folders in the Student's Book.
- If you are not sure of an answer, **write possible answers**, then go on to the other questions in that task. When you have finished the task, go back and choose one answer to each question.
- Check that you have followed the instructions, such as giving only one answer or writing no more than three words.
- If you have spent 20 minutes on the passage without finishing it, try and give a possible answer to each question.
- If you have written on the Reading Module, copy your answers onto the Answer Sheet before going on to the next passage.

READING PASSAGE 1

*You should spend about 20 minutes on **Questions 1–13** which are based on Reading Passage 1 on page 56.*

Questions 1–7

Reading Passage 1 has ten paragraphs **A–J**.

*Choose the correct headings for paragraphs **D–J** from the list of headings below.*

Write the correct number i–x in boxes 1–7 on your answer sheet.

List of Headings
i   Limited success in suppressing the game
ii   Opposition to the role of football in schools
iii   A way of developing moral values
iv   Football matches between countries
v   A game that has survived
vi   Separation into two sports
vii   Proposals for minor improvements
viii Attempts to standardise the game
ix   Probably not an early version of football
x   A chaotic activity with virtually no rules

Example Paragraph **C**	*Answer* v

1	Paragraph **D**
2	Paragraph **E**
3	Paragraph **F**
4	Paragraph **G**
5	Paragraph **H**
6	Paragraph **I**
7	Paragraph **J**

The Origins of Football

A   Football as we now know it developed in Britain in the 19th century, but the game is far older than this. In fact, the term has historically been applied to games played on foot, as opposed to those played on horseback, so 'football' hasn't always involved *kicking* a ball. It has generally been played by men, though at the end of the 17th century, games were played between married and single women in a town in Scotland. The married women regularly won.

B   The very earliest form of football for which we have evidence is the 'tsu'chu', which was played in China and may date back 3,000 years. It was performed in front of the Emperor during festivities to mark his birthday. It involved kicking a leather ball through a 30–40cm opening into a small net fixed onto long bamboo canes – a feat that demanded great skill and excellent technique.

C   Another form of the game, also originating from the Far East, was the Japanese 'kemari', which dates from about the fifth century and is still played today. This is a type of circular football game, a more dignified and ceremonious experience requiring certain skills, but not competitive in the way the Chinese game was, nor is there the slightest sign of struggle for possession of the ball. The players had to pass the ball to each other, in a relatively small space, trying not to let it touch the ground.

D   The Romans had a much livelier game, 'harpastum'. Each team member had his own specific tactical assignment, and the crowds of spectators took a noisy interest in the proceedings and the score. The role of the feet was so small as scarcely to be of consequence. The game remained popular for 700 or 800 years, but, although it was taken to England, it is doubtful whether it can be considered as a forerunner of contemporary football.

E   The game that flourished in Britain from the 8th to the 19th centuries was substantially different from all the previously known forms – more disorganised, more violent, more spontaneous and usually played by an indefinite number of players. Frequently, the games took the form of a heated contest between whole villages. Kicking opponents was allowed, as in fact was almost everything else.

F   There was tremendous enthusiasm for football, even though the authorities repeatedly intervened to restrict it, as a public nuisance. In the 14th and 15th centuries, England, Scotland and France all made football punishable by law, because of the disorder that commonly accompanied it, or because the well-loved recreation prevented subjects from practising more useful military disciplines. None of these efforts had much effect.

G   The English passion for football was particularly strong in the 16th century, influenced by the popularity of the rather better organised Italian game of 'calcio'. English football was as rough as ever, but it found a prominent supporter in the school headmaster Richard Mulcaster. He pointed out that it had positive educational value and promoted health and strength. Mulcaster claimed that all that was needed was to refine it a little, limit the number of participants in each team and, more importantly, have a referee to oversee the game.

H   The game persisted in a disorganised form until the early 19th century, when a number of influential English schools developed their own adaptations. In some, including Rugby School, the ball could be touched with the hands or carried, opponents could be tripped up and even kicked. It was recognised in educational circles that, as a team game, football helped to develop such fine qualities as loyalty, selflessness, co-operation, subordination and deference to the team spirit. A 'games cult' developed in schools, and some form of football became an obligatory part of the curriculum.

I   In 1863, developments reached a climax. At Cambridge University, an initiative began to establish some uniform standards and rules that would be accepted by everyone, but there were essentially two camps: the minority – Rugby School and some others – wished to continue with their own form of the game, in particular allowing players to carry the ball. In October of the same year, eleven London clubs and schools sent representatives to establish a set of fundamental rules to govern the matches played amongst them. This meeting marked the birth of the Football Association.

J   The dispute concerning kicking and tripping opponents and carrying the ball was discussed thoroughly at this and subsequent meetings, until eventually, on 8 December, the die-hard exponents of the Rugby style withdrew, marking a final split between rugby and football. Within eight years, the Football Association already had 50 member clubs, and the first football competition in the world was started – the FA Cup.

Questions 8–13

Complete each sentence with the correct ending **A–I** from the box below.
Write the correct letter **A–I** in boxes 8–13 on your answer sheet.

8 Tsu'chu

9 Kemari

10 Harpastum

11 From the 8th to the 19th centuries, football in the British Isles

12 In the 14th and 15th centuries, the authorities acted on the belief that football

13 In 19th-century England, football

> **A** was seen as something to be encouraged in the young.
> **B** involved individual players having different responsibilities.
> **C** was influenced by a game from another country.
> **D** was a co-operative effort by all the players.
> **E** distracted people from more important activities.
> **F** was played by teams of a fixed size.
> **G** was less popular than it later became.
> **H** was often played by one community against another.
> **I** formed part of a celebration.

You should spend about 20 minutes on **Questions 14–26** which are based on Reading Passage 2 below.

What does the future hold?

The prospects for humanity and for the world as a whole are somewhere between glorious and dire. It is hard to be much more precise.

By 'glorious', I mean that our descendants – all who are born on to this Earth – could live very comfortably and securely, and could continue to do so for as long as the Earth can support life, which should be for a very long time indeed. We should at least be thinking in terms of the next million years. Furthermore, our descendants could continue to enjoy the company of other species – establishing a much better relationship with them than we have now. Other animals need not live in constant fear of us. Many of those fellow species now seem bound to become extinct, but a significant proportion could and should continue to live alongside us. Such a future may seem ideal, and so it is. Yet I do not believe it is fanciful. There is nothing in the physical fabric of the Earth or in our own biology to suggest that this is not possible.

'Dire' means that we human beings could be in deep trouble within the next few centuries, living but also dying in large numbers in political terror and from starvation, while huge numbers of our fellow creatures would simply disappear, leaving only the ones that we find convenient – chickens, cattle – or that we can't shake off, like flies and mice. I'm taking it to be self-evident that glory is preferable.

Our future is not entirely in our own hands because the Earth has its own rules, is part of the solar system and is neither stable nor innately safe. Other planets in the solar system are quite beyond habitation, because their temperature is far too high or too low to be endured, and ours, too, in principle could tip either way. Even relatively unspectacular changes in the atmosphere could do the trick. The core of the Earth is hot, which in many ways is good for living creatures, but every now and again, the molten rock bursts through volcanoes on the surface. Among the biggest volcanic eruptions in recent memory was Mount St Helens, in the USA, which threw out a cubic kilometre of ash – fortunately in an area where very few people live. In 1815, Tambora (in present-day Indonesia) expelled so much ash into the upper atmosphere that climatic effects seriously harmed food production around the world for season after season. Entire civilisations have been destroyed by volcanoes.

Yet nothing we have so far experienced shows what volcanoes can really do. Yellowstone National Park in the USA occupies the caldera (the crater formed when a volcano collapses) of an exceedingly ancient volcano of extraordinary magnitude. Modern surveys show that its centre is now rising. Sometime in the next 200 million years, Yellowstone could erupt again, and when it does, the whole world will be transformed. Yellowstone could erupt tomorrow. But there's a very good chance that it will give us another million years, and that surely is enough to be going on with. It seems sensible to assume that this will be the case.

The universe at large is dangerous, too: in particular, we share the sky with vast numbers of asteroids, and every now and again, they come into our planet's atmosphere. An asteroid the size of a small island, hitting the Earth at 15,000 kilometres an hour (a relatively modest speed by the standards of heavenly bodies), would strike the ocean bed like a rock in a puddle, send a tidal wave around the world as high as a small mountain and as fast as a jumbo jet, and propel us into an ice age that could last for centuries. There are plans to head off such disasters (including rockets to push approaching asteroids into new trajectories), but in truth it's down to luck. On the other hand, the archaeological and the fossil evidence shows that no truly devastating asteroid has struck since the one that seems to have accounted for the extinction of the dinosaurs 65 million years ago. So again, there seems no immediate reason for despair. The Earth is indeed an uncertain place, in an uncertain universe, but with average luck, it should do us well enough. If the world does become inhospitable in the next few thousand or million years, then it will probably be our own fault. In short, despite the underlying uncertainty, our own future and that of our fellow creatures is very much in our own hands.

Given average luck on the geological and the cosmic scale, the difference between glory and disaster will be made, and is being made, by politics. Certain kinds of political systems and strategies would predispose us to long-term survival (and indeed to comfort and security and the pleasure of being alive), while others would take us more and more frenetically towards collapse. The broad point is, though, that we need to look at ourselves – humanity – and at the world in general in a quite new light. Our material problems are fundamentally those of biology. We need to think, and we need our politicians to think, biologically. Do that, and take the ideas seriously, and we are in with a chance. Ignore biology and we and our fellow creatures haven't a hope.

Questions 14–19

Do the following statements reflect the claims of the writer in Reading Passage 2?

In boxes 14–19 on your answer sheet write

YES   *if the statement reflects the claims of the writer*
NO   *if the statement contradicts the claims of the writer*
NOT GIVEN *if it is impossible to say what the writer thinks about this*

14 It seems inevitable that some species will disappear.

15 The nature of the Earth and human biology make it impossible for human beings to survive another million years.

16 An eruption by Yellowstone is likely to be more destructive than previous volcanic eruptions.

17 There is a greater chance of the Earth being hit by small asteroids than by large ones.

18 If the world becomes uninhabitable, it is likely to be as a result of a natural disaster.

19 Politicians currently in power seem unlikely to change their way of thinking.

Questions 20–25

Complete the summary below.
*Choose **NO MORE THAN TWO WORDS** from the passage for each answer.*
Write your answers in boxes 20–25 on your answer sheet.

The Earth could become uninhabitable, like other planets, through a major change in the
20 .... Volcanic eruptions of 21 .... can lead to shortages of 22 ....
in a wide area. An asteroid hitting the Earth could create a 23 .... that would result in a
new 24 .... Plans are being made to use 25 .... to deflect asteroids heading
for the Earth.

Question 26

*Choose the correct letter, **A**, **B**, **C** or **D**.*
Write your answer in box 26 on your answer sheet.

What is the writer's purpose in Reading Passage 2?

A to propose a new theory about the causes of natural disasters
B to prove that generally held beliefs about the future are mistaken
C to present a range of opinions currently held by scientists
D to argue the need for a general change in behaviour

READING PASSAGE 3

You should spend about 20 minutes on **Questions 27–40** which are based on Reading Passage 3 below.

The study of electricity in the 18th century

A In the last two centuries, our lives have been transformed by electricity, although we have been aware of it for far longer: over 2,600 years ago, the Ancient Greeks discovered that rubbing a piece of amber would make feathers stick to it. This was what we now call 'static electricity', which is electricity that does not move. However, the Ancient Greeks couldn't explain the phenomenon or work out how to use it.

B There was little progress until 1600, when the English scientist William Gilbert described the electrification of many substances and coined the term *electricity*, from the Greek word for 'amber'. Attempts were then made to generate usable amounts of static electricity, notably by the German Otto von Guericke. The electrostatic generator that he built in 1660 helped scientists to study electric shocks and sparks.

C In the late 1720s, the British scientist Stephen Gray discovered a way of making static electricity move: electricity produced by applying friction to a glass container could be conducted along a wire to an ivory ball. As a result, the ball behaved as though it had itself been rubbed, attracting paper and other light objects. It is also thought that Gray carried out 'flying boy' experiments: suspending a boy with silk cords and conducting static electricity to his hands so that pieces of paper stuck to them.

D A few years later, the French scientist Charles du Fay (or DuFay) realised that electricity could vary: he in fact identified what we now know as positive and negative charges. He also discovered that opposite charges attract, while similar ones repel each other. Like Gray, du Fay realised that certain materials conducted electricity, while others acted as insulation, stopping the loss of electricity from charged objects.

E Electricity was often thought of as an invisible fluid - du Fay believed two were involved - and attempts were made to collect and store it. In 1746, the Dutchman Pieter van Musschenbroek invented the Leyden (or Leiden) jar, named after the town where he carried out his research. This was a glass container, lined both inside and out with a thin layer of metal and filled with water. It stored static electricity, but could only discharge it all at the same time.

F The American Benjamin Franklin did considerable research into electricity in the 1740s and '50s, and argued against du Fay by proposing a one-fluid model of electricity. His most famous experiment in this area took place in 1752, though the details are disputed. He is thought to have attached a key to a kite - to lift it into the air - and attached the end of the kite string to a Leyden jar. He carried out the experiment when a storm was approaching, and found that the electrified air caused the key to spark, and that electricity travelled along the string into the Leyden jar. This confirmed the suspicion that lightning was actually electricity.

G In the 1780s, the Italian scientist Luigi Galvani carried out a number of experiments on animal electricity. He found that the muscles of a dead frog would move if they were connected to an electrical machine, or if the frog was lying on a metal surface during a thunderstorm. Galvani concluded that the muscles themselves manufactured and stored electricity.

H Not everyone was convinced by his theory. His fellow-countryman Alessandro Volta argued that the electricity was caused by the interaction between water and chemicals in the animal and the metal probes that Galvani had used. He tested his ideas by touching different pairs of metals with his tongue; that way, he could feel tiny electrical currents that could not be detected by the instruments of the time. In order to magnify the currents, he invented the 'voltaic pile' - later to become the modern battery. He was the first person to generate electricity through a chemical reaction.

I The voltaic pile, which Volta publicly demonstrated in 1799, consisted of a number of metal discs, alternately silver and zinc, all of them separated by layers of cardboard. These had previously been saturated in salt water. When the top and bottom discs were connected by means of a wire, a fairly steady current was produced. Volta's invention led to a major step forward in the study of electrical currents. Almost immediately, the Englishman William Nicholson found that the current from such a pile could be used to decompose water into hydrogen and oxygen, the first hint of what a powerful tool for science the invention would soon become. Before long, electricity was replacing animals and steam as the power used to operate machines.

Questions 27–31

Look at the following statements (Questions 27–31) and the list of people below.
Match each statement with the person it describes.
Write the correct letter **A–J** in boxes 27–31 on your answer sheet. **NB** You may use any letter more than once.

27 disagreed with the claim that animals contain electricity
28 discovered that electricity could be made to travel between objects
29 found a way of strengthening electrical currents
30 proposed that electricity could be found in two forms
31 gave electricity its name

List of People

A the Ancient Greeks
B Gilbert
C von Guericke
D Gray
E du Fay
F van Musschenbroek
G Franklin
H Galvani
I Volta
J Nicholson

Questions 32–35

Reading Passage 3 has nine paragraphs labelled **A–I**.
Which paragraph contains the following information?
Write the correct letter **A–I** in boxes 32–35 on your answer sheet.

32 a description of a glass device for storing electricity
33 an outline of an experiment intended to show that human beings could be charged with electricity
34 examples of the application of electrical currents
35 a claim that the theory that electricity consisted of two fluids was wrong

Questions 36–40

Complete the notes below.
Choose **NO MORE THAN ONE WORD** from the passage for each answer.
Write your answers in boxes 36–40 on your answer sheet.

Voltaic pile

* consisted of pile of discs made of two types of **36** ....
* discs separated by pieces of **37** .... soaked in salt water
* linking top and bottom of pile with a **38** .... created a **39** ....
* was soon used to separate **40** .... into constituent elements

Are you: Female? ▭ Male? ▭

Your first language code:

IELTS Reading Answer Sheet

Module taken (shade one box):   Academic ▭   General Training ▭

1	Visetu Shipping	✓ 1 ✗	**21**	✓ 21 ✗
2		2	**22**	22
3	B	3	**23**	23
4		4	**24**	24
5	13th Edition	5	**25**	25
6		6	**26**	26
7	Bristol	7	**27**	27
8		8	**28**	28
9		9	**29**	29
10		10	**30**	30
11		11	**31**	31
12		12	**32**	32
13		13	**33**	33
14		14	**34**	34
15		15	**35**	35
16		16	**36**	36
17		17	**37**	37
18		18	**38**	38
19	Cato	19	**39**	39
20		20	**40**	40

Checker's Initials		Marker's Initials		Band Score		Reading Total	

Answer key

UNIT 1

Reading

2 1 C *One of the techniques of writing successfully in an academic environment ... you must have a clear picture of what you have read ... Yet many academic texts are densely written in unfamiliar ways*

   2 E *Although sometimes there may be reasons why you need to skim-read an article or book ... skim-reading is not a particularly useful strategy for a student ... Instead of skim-reading, ...*

   3 B *you will need to decide what type of location and atmosphere suits you best, and establish conditions that are conducive to effective study.*

   4 A *... choosing their reading ... consult the reading list ... Doing a library search ... Your tutor should be able to advise you ...*

3 1 entails   2 maintain a constant grip on
   3 the gist   4 in other contexts   5 large chunks
   6 making sense of   7 suits you best   8 conducive
   9 stumbling block   10 on loan

Vocabulary

4 periodical, electronic, search, shelf, card, issue, resources, journal, spine, loan, code(s)

S	W	A	G	L	E	Y	M	I	Z
P	E	R	I	O	D	I	C	A	L
I	N	E	O	A	R	B	O	S	T
N	E	S	F	N	D	J	S	R	O
E	L	E	C	T	R	O	N	I	C
B	O	L	S	E	A	R	C	H	O
A	S	H	E	L	F	C	A	R	D
I	S	S	U	E	V	O	T	L	E
N	R	E	S	O	U	R	C	E	S
J	O	U	R	N	A	L	A	V	O

5 1 electronic search   2 code   3 spine
   4 periodical/journal   5 journal/periodical
   6 issue   7 loan   8 card   9 resources   10 shelf

Grammar

6 1 mustn't   2 should   3 haven't   4 had to
   5 might   6 needs to   7 couldn't   8 may
7 1 couldn't/can't have   2 must have
   3 could/may/might have   4 could/may/might have
   5 can't/couldn't have   6 couldn't/can't have

UNIT 2

Reading

2 1 *doping has become irresistible to many athletes, if only to keep pace with competitors who are doing it.* (lines 8–10)
   2 *Where victory is paramount, athletes will seize any opportunity* (lines 10–12)
   3 *Sports authorities fear that a new form of doping will be undetectable and thus much less preventable.* (lines 14–15)
   4 *Treatments that regenerate muscle, increase its strength and protect it from degradation will soon be entering human clinical trials for muscle-wasting disorders.* (lines 16–19)
   5 *it is also a dream come true for an athlete bent on doping.* (lines 25–26)
   6 *The chemicals are indistinguishable from their natural counterparts* (lines 26–27)
   7 *the world may be about to watch one of its final Olympic Games without genetically enhanced athletes.* (lines 36–38)

Vocabulary

3 1 synthetic   2 counterparts   3 certainly
   4 detect   5 irresistible   6 treatments
   7 degradation   8 manipulating   9 scandals
(The vertical word is *specimens*.)

Grammar

4 1 has been struggling / has struggled
   2 has David been playing   3 has signed
   4 Have you set   5 have been trying
   6 hadn't expected   7 Has the college entered
   8 has won

5 **1** As the information age **has** arrived, people's work and lives have **become / are becoming** more and more dependent on computers.

2 It has **been happening** for the past two weeks, at the same time every evening.

3 I used my lighter to light the candle but unfortunately I've also lit a book I **had just been reading**!

4 We **had** been / **were** waiting for 20 minutes before someone came to give us a menu.

5 The computer is one of those inventions that **has** changed the way we live.

6 *correct*

7 There **have been** recent cases in other sports events in which people have injured themselves because of unsafe equipment.

6 **1** … Ian Thorp had broken the world record for the 50m freestyle earlier today.

2 … Rusedski had been cleared of drug-taking and the charges against him dropped.

3 … builders had almost completed work on the new stadium.

UNIT 3

Reading

2 **1** NG The article says that *Skoda owners couldn't claim to be leaders of fashion* (line 7), but we aren't told if any makes of car were less popular.

2 NG *the Czech government, Skoda's owner, decided the business needed foreign investment. In 1991, it went into partnership with the German car manufacturer Volkswagen* (lines 10–13). We aren't told if the government negotiated with other companies as well.

3 Y *Although motoring journalists were generally positive about it, UK sales were poor* (lines 17–18): the word *although* shows that the writer thinks sales should have been better.

4 N *the company still had an out-dated image that no longer matched its products* (lines 25–26) – so the Octavia *didn't* seem out-dated.

5 N *In the UK, Skoda at least had the advantage of high 'brand awareness' – that is, many people recognised the name* (lines 33–35).

6 NG The Fabia was more successful than the other two models, but the writer doesn't compare their quality.

7 Y *for many UK customers, a Skoda is a cut-price Volkswagen* (lines 44–45)

Grammar

3 **1** the Fabia   **2** in the 1980s
3 at the end of the century   **4** the Felicia
5 that the business needed foreign investment
6 the fact that the company's costs had increased
7 high 'brand awareness'

4 **1** D   **2** G   **3** C   **4** F   **5** B   **6** A

Vocabulary

5 **1** logo   **2** Competition   **3** goods   **4** launch
5 consumer   **6** Marketing   **7** purchase   **8** image
9 service   **10** retail

UNIT 4

Vocabulary

1 **1** acronyms   **2** Nonverbal communication
3 slang   **4** idiom   **5** collocations   **6** jargon

Grammar

2 Time: after, as, as soon as, before, once, since, until, when, whenever, while
Place: where, wherever
Reason: as, because, since
Purpose: so that
Condition: even if, if, unless
Concession: although, even if, even though, though, whereas, while

3 **1** *when they were first coined* (lines 30–31)

2 *When a football manager, asked how he felt about the defeat of his team, said that he was* as sick as a parrot, *a reference to the sensational cases of psittacosis from West Africa in the early 1970s* (lines 32–36)

3 *until the cows come home* (lines 44–45)

4 *if you deny us the use of cliché.* (lines 49–50)

5 *because they are the best way of saying something.* (lines 57–58)

6 *if you denied yourself the use of the brightest, most economical and most beautiful phrases invented, simply because they were clichés.* (lines 61–64)

7 *because they were clichés.* (lines 63–64) (Note that this reason clause is contained within the time clause in 6.)

8 *if it is the best way of saying what I want to say.* (lines 67–68)

Reading

5 **1** G   **2** D   **3** B   **4** H   **5** E   **6** A

UNIT 5

Reading

2 **1** conventional   **2** interact with   **3** reaction
4 impregnated with   **5** optimal concentrations
6 inner layer

Vocabulary

3 **1** prevent   **2** track   **3** introduce   **4** stay
5 cause   **6** consume   **7** control
(The vertical word is *protect*.)

Grammar

4 **1** can/may be kept   **2** are made   **3** was invented
4 to be used   **5** has been found   **6** are related
5 **1** More goods are being produced in plastic.
2 A plastics recycling scheme has just been
introduced by our local council.
3 Plastics are used in the manufacture of pills.
4 A new type of biodegradable plastic bottle is
about to be launched.
5 The factory's glassmaking division might be shut
down, to concentrate on plastic.
6 If plastic hadn't been invented, what materials
would be being used today?

UNIT 6

Reading

2 **1** C *the problem with focus groups is … the moment
the anthropologist's presence is known, everything
changes … any experimental group wants to
please the examiner. For focus groups, this is
particularly true.* (lines 24–30)
2 C *I've found that every time we make a few songs
available on my website, sales of all the CDs go
up.* (lines 35–37)
3 B *So I make most of my living from live touring …
I spend hours each week doing press, writing
articles, making sure my website tour
information is up to date.* (lines 49–53)
4 D *Here's a fool-proof way to deliver music to
millions who might otherwise never purchase a
CD in a store.* (lines 57–59)
5 A *Most of all, I'd like to see an end to the hysteria
that causes a group like the RIAA to spend over
45 million dollars in 2001 lobbying 'on our
behalf', when every record company out there is
complaining that they have no money.*
(lines 74–77)

Grammar

3 **1** despite the fact
2 In spite of (his) being
3 whereas Metallica do/does
4 even though I have / I've

Vocabulary

4

Noun	Adjective	Adverb
realism	realistic, real	realistically
artist	artistic	artistically
technology	technological	technologically
finance	financial	financially
meaning	meaningless	meaninglessly
effect	effective	effectively
prediction	unpredictable	unpredictably
universe	universal	universally
science, scientist	scientific	scientifically
manipulation	manipulative	manipulatively

5 **1** excited   **2** gloomy   **3** cheerful   **4** light-hearted
5 emotional

UNIT 7

Reading

2 **1** D *When we're presented with a puzzle, … we work
until we find a solution. In fact, we intentionally
set ourselves such problems, like crossword
puzzles* (lines 15–21)
2 G *it seems rather unlikely that our salaries are the
sole motivation.* (lines 25–27)
3 A *We childproof our houses and say, with a sigh,
that the baby is 'always getting into things'.*
(lines 36–38)
4 I *they venture out to explore and then, in a sudden
panic, race back to the safe haven, only to venture
forth again some few minutes later.* (lines 47–51)
5 B *the dangers of exploration are offset by the
benefits of learning.* (lines 60–61)
6 E *they will quite systematically explore the way one
object can influence another object* (lines 98–101)
3 **1** laboratories   **2** attention   **3** cloth   **4** rake
5 explanations

Vocabulary

4 **1** take **2** carried out **3** testing **4** promote
5 make **6** sought **7** shape **8** underlie
9 endangered **10** offset

Style Extra

5 **1** It appears to be the case that we are driven to ensure the success and continuation of not just our own genes, but of the species.
2 It was asserted by Copernicus in 1530 that the Earth rotates on its axis once a day and travels round the sun once a year.
3 Most people in the 16th century found it hard to believe that the planets orbit round the sun.
4 It is unlikely that a large comet or asteroid will hit the Earth.
5 Radio telescopes have made it possible (for us) to extend our knowledge of the universe.
6 It will take a great deal of time, effort and money (for us) to establish settlements on the moon.

UNIT 8

Writing

1 *Possible answer*
Terms of reference
This report is intended to highlight problems currently faced by the Kitchen of the Future Research Unit.
Physical environment
The Unit is based in an annex of the company's head office. However, the facilities are out-of-date, and the offices are full of reports, equipment, etc. Staff are sometimes unable to find specific information that they are asked for, as the relevant report cannot be located. It is therefore likely that unless the Unit moves to more spacious and better-equipped premises very soon, it will be unable to continue operations.
Work of the Unit
The Unit produces a large number of reports on innovations affecting the food industry. Reports are commissioned by outside bodies, and staff travel anywhere in the world to carry out the necessary research. They are so experienced that they can produce a report in a very short time.

Staff also work on projects to invent new products, most recently the 'Music Knife', a gadget which optimises cooking preparations by playing music of a suitable mood and speed.

Grammar

2 **1** H **2** D **3** G **4** B **5** A **6** E **7** C **8** J
9 F **10** I

Reading

4 **1** F *growth has mainly been concentrated at the upper end of the market … consumers trade up* (lines 4–7)
2 T *The major sector within built-in appliances is cooking … with 79% by volume. Within the free-standing market, cooking takes 28% by volume* (lines 8–11)
3 T *gas has made some gains in share* (lines 18–19)
4 NG We are told proportions (65% and 59%), but not the numbers of appliances sold.
5 T *The built-in cooking market has experienced considerable growth in terms of volume, and this has spread to increased demand for extractor hoods.* (lines 24–27)
6 F *growth potential still exists.* (line 31)
7 NG We are told they have a 55% share, not whether that proportion has changed.
8 NG Although 55% of all free-standing cookers use gas, the proportion isn't necessarily the same for range cookers.
9 F *significant growth within the fridge/freezer sector.* (lines 45–46)
10 T *The wider product range … contributed to growth in this sector.* (lines 50–54)

UNIT 9

Reading

2 **1** T *'I wonder if we could do this in Buenos Aires,' said a wide-eyed Horacio Blot* (lines 9–10)
2 T *Ministers of transport, mayors of capital cities and representatives from NGOs met at the event* (lines 15–16)
3 F *Misión Bogotá, a programme whereby marginalised citizens and petty criminals are given jobs* (lines 22–23)
4 T *he managed to reduce homicide by a staggering 40% in 1996* (lines 26–27)
5 F *Construction of the stunning municipal library that hosted the conference also began under Peñalosa* (lines 37–38)
6 F *Michael Replogle of the United States NGO Environmental Defense said, 'While I have long advocated bus rapid-transit strategies …* (lines 48–50)

3 **1** NG **2** ✓ **3** ✓ **4** ✓ **5** NG **6** ✓

Vocabulary

4 1 e 2 c 3 f 4 b 5 a 6 g 7 h 8 d

Writing

5 1 One 2 another 3 a third 4 not only
  5 but also 6 Among 7 Alongside 8 thus

Grammar

6 1 Ben could scarcely have known about the road closures as he doesn't drive.
  2 The traffic lights had no sooner turned green before they went back to red again.
  3 I have rarely visited as beautiful a city as Ljubljana, the capital of Slovenia.
  4 I hardly need to add that all mobile phones should now be switched off.
  OR I need hardly to add that all mobile phones should now be switched off.
  5 There was barely enough room for everyone who boarded the bus.

UNIT 10

Reading

2 1 D *our welcome would have been short-lived had we not scrupulously observed their time-hallowed rituals and taboos.* (lines 17–19)
  2 C *We also sought out the dreamers named by Stewart in his PhD thesis, finding two of them still living and interviewing the families of others. Sadly, we must report that no one recalled any form of dream-control education in childhood or any such practice amongst adults; in fact, they vehemently denied that dream manipulation has ever been part of their culture.* (lines 22–28)
  3 D *the 'gunig', or protective spirit, always chooses its human vehicle* (lines 42–43)
  4 B *they emphatically denied that it played any part in their tradition.* (lines 57–58)
  5 A *we feel we must put a ban on the misuse of their name, which proponents of dream control seem reluctant to do.* (lines 60–62)

Vocabulary

3

Grammar

4 1 Could my bad dream last night have been due to that cheese I ate?
  My bad dream last night couldn't have been due to that cheese I ate, could it?
  2 The fact that you cannot remember your dreams might be reversible, mightn't it?
  Mightn't your inability to remember dreams be reversible?
  3 David's dream couldn't have been caused by watching that film.
  There's no way that David's dream could have been caused by watching that film.

UNIT 11

Reading

2 1 iii 2 viii 3 vi 4 v 5 i

Vocabulary

3 1 collapse of the volcano
  2 evacuation of the residents
  3 destruction of Akrotiri
  4 evidence of habitation
  5 (some) speculation
  6 Akrotiri's prosperity
4 1 compelling 2 scientific 3 fundamental
  4 physical 5 full-blown

Grammar

5 **1** Situated **2** dating **3** based **4** to meet
5 leaving **6** to find **7** to be

6 *-ing* forms: leaving (line 5), consisting (line 6),
going (line 17), containing (line 25), reaching (line
29), producing (line 33)
-ed forms: centred (line 19), removed (line 31)
infinitives: to be forced (lines 9–10), to have brought
(line 40), to have been evacuated (lines 42–43)

UNIT 12

Reading

2 **1** C *an array of subjects: astronomy, medicine,
mathematics, chemistry, judicial law, government
and Islamic conflict resolution.*

2 G *the manuscripts of Timbuktu are beginning to be
re-catalogued, preserved and protected against
theft.*

3 B *Timbuktu, in present-day Mali, West Africa*

4 G *With the pressures of poverty and a series of
droughts, many manuscripts have been sold
illegally to private collectors abroad.*

5 A *Scholars and students travelled from as far away
as Cairo, Baghdad and Persia to study from the
noted manuscripts found in the town.*

6 B *An integral part of Timbuktu's history was
always trade – the exchange of salt that came
from the heart of the Sahara. To this day, camel
caravans laden with salt, also known as 'the gold
of the desert', journey to Timbuktu*

7 E *By the beginning of the 1600s, however, partly
because of invasions, the scholars of Timbuktu
had slowly begun to drift away and study
elsewhere … scholastic study fell off sharply with
the French colonisation of the region in the late
1890s.*

8 C *Accompanying the camel caravans rode the
scholars of Islamic learning, bringing with them
over the centuries hundreds of thousands of
manuscripts.*

3 **1** scholars / 'ambassadors of peace'
2 camel caravans **3** disrepair **4** (mud) homes
5 Timbuktu Heritage Institute
6 World Heritage Site

Grammar

4 **1** to have inherited **2** to be seen **3** to have had
4 to have completed **5** to be improving
6 to be found **7** to have been taken
8 to be remembered **9** to have been walking
10 to be happening

Vocabulary

5 **1** f **2** c **3** e **4** a **5** g **6** d **7** b **8** h
6 **b** put on your earphones now.
f take several new trainees on.

UNIT 13

Reading

2 **1** collision **2** destruction **3** research
4 suggestion **5** device **6** data **7** nature
8 core **9** risk **10** action **11** effect **12** shift
13 result **14** force

Grammar

3 **1** will be passing / will pass **2** will be affected
3 will be travelling; won't remain
4 will be learned/learnt **5** will never be
6 will be altered

Vocabulary

4 **1** causing **2** hazards **3** impact **4** orbit
5 outcome **6** proximity **7** implications
(The horizontal word is *gravitational.*)

UNIT 14

Reading

2 **1** (social) expectations **2** significant phenomenon
3 voting patterns **4** consumer choice
5 (social) status

Vocabulary

3 **1** unprecedented **2** overriding **3** penetrating
4 materialistic **5** radical **6** fundamental
7 autonomous **8** atypical
4 **1** fundamental **2** penetrating **3** atypical
4 overriding **5** radical **6** autonomous

Grammar

5　1　When we exercise, we know that **it** is difficult to avoid such a situation.

　2　There are a lot more questions that we require answers to before **we** can reach a verdict on such an important issue.

　3　Finally, good relationships with the people around **us** is another factor in how far we achieve happiness.

　4　Rich countries should take more responsibility for helping the poorer **ones**.

　5　Maybe for other people these things are not so important, but for me **they** are very important.

　6　In my essay, **I** discuss the merits and demerits of the mobile phone.

　7　Considering that Australia is a good place for jobs, **this/it** is quite an alarming trend.

6　1　All; which　2　each other　3　myself　4　ours
　5　who　6　these; somewhere　7　it　8　those
　9　neither　10　someone; whom

UNIT 15

Reading

2　1　B　*It is our hope that you will leave the site with a broader appreciation of the relationship of medicine to culture* (lines 9–10)

　2　A　*Cycles of fevers and chills may be identified as being a particular disease, part of a general pattern of seasonal health or an internal struggle of opposing yet complementary forces. These are more than just descriptions; they influence the actual experience of having illness* (lines 18–23)

　3　D　*Our aim is to help you understand why blood-letting, for instance, now considered unacceptable, was a rational and sensible healing activity in the early 19th century.* (lines 39–41)

　4　D　*… we should feel empowered to demand that medicine be responsive to current human needs.* (lines 54–55)

　5　B　*it is easy to read the history of medicine as one of constant progression, leading from barbaric roots to a sophisticated and universally correct scientific approach as embodied in current medical practice. We believe that this notion is problematic.* (lines 56–60) (Remember that the question is about what assumption is criticised.)

Vocabulary

3　1　a website
　2　pain
　3　an illness (*a battle* is also possible)
　4　medicine
　5　the world
　6　an illness (*pain* is also possible)
　7　values (*approach*, *assumptions* and *context* are also possible)
　8　context (*approach* and *light* are also possible)
　9　light (*approach* and *context* are also possible)
　10　approach (*context* and *light* are also possible)
　11　assumptions (*values* is also possible)
　12　judgements

4　1　experience　2　diagnose　3　treat　4　appreciate
　5　relate　6　practise (*AmE* practice)
　7　complement　8　assume　9　respond
　10　progress

5　1　resistance　2　perception　3　assumptions
　4　consultation　5　assessment　6　Failure

UNIT 16

Writing

1　1　force　2　undergo　3　play　4　points　5　key
　6　responds　7　established

Vocabulary

2　1　conscious　2　pragmatic　3　inference
　4　soluble　5　equivalent　6　investigate　7　entity
　8　complementary

Reading

4　1　D　*Penrose has suggested that consciousness involves physical principles not yet understood. Perhaps the flesh-and-blood brain has the chemistry required to use the physics required to produce consciousness, while silicon chips lack this ability?* (lines 91–98)

　2　A　*Turing showed that a machine's ability to compute does not depend on what it is made of. All that matters is that the parts of the machine should be arranged appropriately.* (lines 39–44)

　3　F　*One is the 'dualism' of René Descartes (1596–1650), which says the universe has two components – matter (that is, physical substance or material) and mind.* (lines 108–113)

4 C *as the British zoologist Sir Peter Medawar commented, science is merely 'the art of the soluble'. Science answers only those questions that scientists ask and which they are technically able to investigate.* (lines 68–74)

5 B *As the American philosopher John Searle has pointed out, it is possible to make computers that imitate all kinds of human thinking, but that does not mean they think as we do. An imitation of consciousness does not necessarily show consciousness.* (lines 31–38)

6 A *Turing pointed out that it is impossible to know whether other human beings are conscious.* (lines 11–14)

UNIT 17

Vocabulary

2 **1** T *Temperatures below 55°F make it impossible for them to take to the air* (lines 6–7)

2 T *flying with the wind to reach their winter homes.* (line 11)

3 NG The passage states how many butterflies migrate to California and Mexico, but not the proportions to each country.

4 F *They cluster in pine and eucalyptus trees along the California coast* (lines 17–18)

5 T *The weight of the cluster also prevents the butterflies from being blown away.* (lines 22–23)

6 NG The passage states that the butterflies stay in their winter homes until about March, but does not say whether this is shorter than before.

7 F *travelling as fast as 30mph at times.* (lines 25–26)

8 T *Monarch butterflies are in danger of losing both their summer and winter habitats. Summer habitats are being destroyed as more roads and new housing developments and business complexes encroach upon open space* (lines 27–30)

9 T *the butterfly larvae … feed on this plant alone.* (lines 32–33)

10 NG The passage refers to the logging in Mexico exposing the butterflies to life-threatening elements, but does not refer to mortality rates.

Vocabulary

3 **1** latitude **2** phenomenon **3** orientation
4 migration **5** site **6** track **7** adjustment
8 landmark **9** anomalies
(The word vertically is *longitude*, relating to *latitude*.)

Writing

4 *Suggested answer*
The population of Ireland, which reached about 8.5 million by 1845, had increased dramatically in the first half of the 19th century. Irish peasants, who depended on the potato as their single food crop, favoured a variety called 'Aran Banner'. This potato was susceptible to a disease known as 'potato blight', which had spread from North America to Europe. The Irish Potato Famine, which was caused by a total crop failure, took hold in the winter of 1845–46. Irish towns and cities, where hundreds of thousands of starving people went for relief, became ridden with diseases such as typhoid and cholera. In 1848, when the potato crop failed once again, there was a further outbreak of cholera. Over 1.5 million people who left Ireland in the late 1840s emigrated to Britain or North America.

UNIT 18

Vocabulary

1 1 unpredictable 2 underfunded
3 ill-informed/misinformed/uninformed
4 impossible 5 impractical 6 ill-considered
7 invalid
2 1 underfunded 2 invalid 3 unpredictable
4 impossible
3 1 d 2 a 3 b
4 1 is a real can of worms
2 has caused / is causing a complete storm
3 has a hidden agenda

Grammar

5 discover, estimate, show, plan, doubt, (speculate,)
describe, assess, consider, remind, reflect, realise,
evaluate

S	D	I	S	C	O	V	E	R	N
P	E	S	T	I	M	A	T	E	E
E	S	A	O	C	R	R	R	S	V
C	C	S	H	O	W	E	E	S	A
U	R	S	C	N	R	F	A	I	L
L	I	E	S	S	E	L	L	H	U
A	B	S	U	I	M	E	I	R	A
T	E	S	U	D	I	C	S	L	T
E	X	E	R	E	N	T	E	E	E
P	L	A	N	R	D	O	U	B	T

6 1 remind 2 describes/shows
3 showing/reflecting 4 doubt 5 discover
6 assess/evaluate/discover 7 realises/discovers
8 plans
7 1 (has) estimated what / (has) estimated how big
2 is advising him which / advised him which
3 is asking whether / asked whether
4 hasn't found out who / didn't manage to find out
who
5 is suggesting how / suggested how
6 is questioning whether / questioned whether

UNIT 19

Reading

1 1 viii *you may be experiencing increasing pressure to
stay late at night, take work home or just 'pop
into the office' at the weekend ... you find the
boundaries between life and work beginning to
blur ... finding your job satisfying does not
make you want to spend all your time at work
either*
2 i *Andre discusses his canoe-polo commitments
with his line manager, who does his best to
build them into the work schedule.*
3 vi *The workplace in Australia, as in many other
countries, is significantly different from what it
was not all that long ago. It needs a more
flexible, skilled and responsive workforce. At the
same time, employees are increasingly looking
for flexible working conditions*
4 ii *it's a win-win situation. The employee has
greater flexibility, and the employer is rewarded
with greater commitment, higher staff morale
and reduced absenteeism.*
5 v *work/life balance is less gender specific and
recognises other commitments as well as family.*
2 1 enjoy 2 reconsider 3 train 4 accommodate
5 require 6 benefit

Vocabulary

3 2 caters 3 applied/apply 4 appoint
5 qualified 6 refurbished 7 experienced
8 supplies 9 profitable
4 2 current 3 perception 4 promotion
5 expectations 6 disappointment 7 desire
8 reduction 9 anxiety 10 retirement
11 fulfilment/fulfillment

UNIT 20

Reading

2 **1** E *With less religious pressure and greater equality between the sexes in the last few decades, men and women have often worn similar clothes.*

2 B *Articles of clothing were first used in this way as symbols of rank, authority or occupation, … for instance, a king's crown, a bishop's mitre and cope, special robes for judges and the whole range of uniforms for military or specialised services.*

3 D *dress has been used to accentuate good points and disguise shortcomings.*

4 A *Fashion, whether in art, architecture, furniture or dress, must rather be seen as the expression of ideas shared by a number of people at any one time … dress should be regarded as an art form*

5 C *Fashion in clothing is therefore an expression of the communal ideas or beliefs of a social group, and changes in society often lead to new styles.*

6 E *However, most upper- and middle-class women … had for practical reasons to look for social advancement or financial stability in a husband … and this may have encouraged what has been referred to as the seduction principle in women's dress, with a constant change of emphasis on different parts of the anatomy to stimulate interest and attention.*

7 C *even those who choose to dress 'out of fashion' in what they consider a more aesthetic manner and those who are negligent or even slovenly often achieve a sense of superiority in being unconventional.*

3 **1** creative   **2** random   **3** prevailing   **4** affluent
5 manual   **6** rebellious

4 **1** roles   **2** privileged   **3** marriage   **4** attention
5 equality

Grammar

5 **1** would   **2** may   **3** can't   **4** shouldn't
5 wouldn't   **6** could   **7** must   **8** should
9 couldn't   **10** may not

Vocabulary

6 **1** ambition, dream   **2** forestall, prevent
3 outcome, result   **4** distortion, misrepresentation
5 misconception, mistake   **6** impartial, unbiased
7 comprehension, understanding   **8** follow, replace

WRITING WORKOUT 1

1 **1** Y **2** Y **3** N (Try to use other words than those given in the task.) **4** Y **5** N (Use sufficient paragraphing to make your ideas clear.)
6 N (Use only a few rhetorical questions, as they are more effective if used sparingly.) **7** Y **8** Y

2 Relevant sentences: A, C, E, F, G, H, J

3 **1** H **2** A **3** G **4** C **5** E **6** J

4 **1** Some brands are now available globally because companies are investing in international sales and marketing campaigns.
2 Although Coca-Cola is popular everywhere, many local soft drinks are popular, too.
3 Unless international brands are marketed competently, they may not sell worldwide. OR International brands may not sell worldwide unless they are marketed competently.
4 When international brands are advertised locally, their adverts must conform to local expectations.
5 If identity is partly defined by what we buy, it is also influenced by our relationships.

5 **1** Although **2** extremely **3** could
4 in my opinion **5** outlined

6 To **conclude**, it is **definitely** the case that global brands are **increasingly** present in the **lives** of many **people** around the world, but they do not **necessarily** threaten a person's identity. **Personally**, what I find of greater concern is the **likely effect** on local **culture** and customs.

WRITING WORKOUT 2

1 **1** as **2** this/so **3** to **4** of **5** as **6** In
7 not **8** all

2 **1** technologically **2** meaningless **3** manipulative
4 Realistically **5** artistic **6** unpredictably
7 effectively **8** Financially

3 The writer agrees with the statement.

4 **1** B **2** C **3** A **4** C **5** A **6** B **7** C **8** A
9 C **10** B

5 **1** to be made **2** should not be relied
3 (being) prepared **4** are (being) threatened

6 Sample answer
Large potatoes should be chosen for this recipe. Having been washed and dried, each potato should be rubbed with salt and olive oil. The potatoes are then placed on a baking tray and put into a hot oven for about 55 minutes. After the potatoes have been removed from the oven, they should be cut in half lengthwise. The flesh of the potato is scooped out with a spoon, with a thin shell being left inside the skin. The potato flesh is mashed with a fork and can be combined with a range of additional ingredients, such as grated cheese, chopped tomatoes and fresh parsley or coriander. The potato shells are stuffed with the mixture and are then returned to the oven and baked for a further 20 minutes.

WRITING WORKOUT 3

1 **1** Y **2** N (Write 160 words at most.) **3** Y
4 N (Try to include an opening sentence that explains the subject matter.) **5** Y **6** N (Write about trends rather than giving detailed figures.)

2 **1** somewhat **2** exactly **3** entirely **4** rather

3 **1** T **2** T **3** T **4** F (Read the vertical axis information carefully, as each graph is slightly different.) **5** T **6** T **7** F (The rise is predicted to be slightly more gradual, but there is no levelling-off shown.) **8** T

4 **1** bar **2** line **3** accounting **4** higher/more
5 over **6** 2010 **7** double **8** lower/ less
9 opposed **10** level

5 Sample answer
Information is given on the actual and estimated energy consumption and emissions for Australia and South Korea for the period 2002 to 2025. The pie charts show that, currently, both countries consume the same amounts of energy, in spite of the fact that the population of South Korea is more than double that of Australia. At present, each country contributes 1.9% to global carbon-dioxide emissions, but this represents 9.5 tonnes per capita in South Korea, whereas in Australia, the figure is 21 tonnes per capita.
Fuel consumption is forecast to increase in each country, although after 2010, the rise in Australia will be slightly more gradual than South Korea's. As far as carbon-dioxide emissions are concerned, South Korea had a lower level than Australia in 2002, but by 2025, its emissions are expected to have topped 700 million tonnes, whereas in Australia, emissions are likely to rise to just over 600 million tonnes.
(153 words)

WRITING WORKOUT 4

1   In the Academic **Writing** Module, you only have an hour to complete the two tasks. Make sure you leave **enough** time to give yourself the **opportunity** to check both your answers **thoroughly**. Make any **corrections** neatly and **legibly**. Errors often occur when a letter is silent, for example in the words *government*, *technology* and *otherwise*. Be **especially careful** with vowel combinations in words such as *beautiful* and *enormous*. Also, remember to check that you have added any suffixes **accurately**: *-ness* and *-ful* are often misspelled.

2   **Health and illness**

A   People **rarely used to have** as long a life expectancy as we enjoy today. *or* **Rarely did people used to have** as long a life expectancy as we enjoy today.

F   Thanks to advances in modern medicine, we are **better protected** from deadly diseases nowadays.

H   We have to consider **what the causes of this obesity and heart disease are**.

Personal risk-taking and accidents

D   It is true that people **choose to take risks sometimes in their choice of leisure activities**. *or* It is true that people **sometimes choose to take risks in their choice of leisure activities**.

E   **Today**, we are undoubtedly at risk of injury from the cars we drive, a threat that **was absent in the past**.

I   In fact, we are far more likely **to injure ourselves in the home** than outside, which has probably always been the case.

Crime

B   The streets of our cities **now are probably safer** to walk in than they were a hundred years ago. *or* **Now**, the streets … *or* The streets of our cities are probably **safer to walk in now** than …

J   Newspapers and television are partly responsible for the current perception of risk from violent attacks. (*correct*)

Catastrophic events

C   Modern inventions like nuclear power plants could be perceived as life-threatening, although in reality, a dangerous incident is extremely unlikely to occur. (*correct*)

G   Natural disasters such as earthquakes have **always been** a part of life, though it could be argued that we are now facing disasters on a larger scale, due to severe weather trends.

3   1   One year later, the company **sent** me on a merchandising training session.

2   In my essay, I **(will) discuss** the merits and demerits of the mobile phone.

3   I **will be** glad to welcome you and your family next week.

4   Our parents ~~have~~ respected their teachers more than we do.

5   It is a pity that there are so many students who have enrolled in the university but **live** with their family.

6   Before computers, if you **wanted** to write something, you had to write it with a pen or pencil.

7   I've now been to some of the places **I'd been dreaming / I'd dreamt / I dreamt** of as a child.

8   Last week, they **held** a family meeting where they decided they would watch TV for only three hours a day.

9   Parents feel that if their child **becomes** an artist, it will be difficult for him or her financially.

10   Nowadays man **is** influenced by scientific inventions.

4   1   The **lowest** percentage of tourists was ten.

2   Your **prompt** action will be appreciated.

3   Nevertheless, her general condition is still **poor** and requires special care.

4   The least **popular** activities were hobbies.

5   Computers have a vast number of uses in the **modern** world.

6   The chart shows the amount spent on six consumer **goods** in four European countries.

7   I work in an organisation where the office **hours** are from nine to six.

8   Some **scenes** in films are unsuitable for children.

9   Our country has received a lot of aid to help maintain our infrastructure, health **facilities** and agricultural schemes.

10   They depended on old **methods** of communication like drum-beating and lighting fires.

11   Children should be taught that they have responsibility for the **effects** of their actions.

12   I've also been in charge of price **negotiations** with our partners.

13   There is a proposal to hold art **events** in public places.

14   The benefits of computers are greater than the **drawbacks**.

15   In 1980, the **numbers** of scientists and technicians in developing countries was three times smaller than in industrialised countries.

5 Sample answer

In my opinion, it is hard to accept the statement as it stands. While it is true that we face new risks in today's world, we are far healthier than our ancestors, which argues against the statement.

People rarely used to have as long a life expectancy as we enjoy today. Thanks to modern medicine, we are better protected from deadly diseases nowadays. At the same time, bad diet and lack of exercise could be threatening our health by causing obesity and heart disease.

Furthermore, we are undoubtedly at risk of injury from the cars we drive, a threat that was absent in the past. Modern transportation and increased mobility do pose new dangers for us, though minimally so. It is also true that people sometimes choose to take risks in their choice of leisure activities – going sky-diving and bungee-jumping, for example. Yet in fact, we are far more likely to injure ourselves in the home than outside, which has probably always been the case.

Considering the aspect of crime, the streets of our cities are probably safer to walk in now than they were a hundred years ago. Many people today have an irrational fear of crime. Newspapers and television are partly responsible for the current perception of risk from violent attacks.

Finally, how real is the threat of catastrophic events in today's world? Modern inventions like nuclear power plants could be perceived as life-threatening, although in reality, a major incident is extremely unlikely. Natural disasters such as earthquakes have always been a part of life, though it could be argued that we are now facing disasters on a larger scale, due to severe weather trends.

In a nutshell, the argument works both ways. There are new risks associated with our modern lifestyle, though in other ways we are 'safer' than our forebears.

(304 words)

WRITING WORKOUT 5

1 Appropriate features: 1, 2, 3, 5, 7
2 1 rather; suggests   2 little   3 somewhat; so
 4 Perhaps; should   5 a number of   6 a little
 7 it is likely that   8 It cannot be denied
 9 is meant   10 It is absolutely right to suggest, as the writer does, that
3 1 f   2 e   3 c   4 g   5 b   6 a   7 d
4 1 labour   2 complaining   3 pause   4 exploited
 5 behave   6 spent
5 Sample answer

It appears the statement is a little flawed, because even in today's uncertain times, it is still possible to find both satisfaction and security in many areas of current employment. Moreover, it is slightly irrational to suggest that one aspect is more important than the other, given that they are so different. It is a rather meaningless generalisation to make, in any case.

It goes without saying that, for some individuals, long-term job prospects are crucial, perhaps because they are having to spend considerable sums of money each month and need to be confident in their ongoing ability to find the funds. On the other hand, for those people who have fewer personal commitments or are generally more flexible, security will be less of an issue.

What is more, job satisfaction is something that is rather difficult to measure. It cannot be denied that the majority of people would prefer to do a job that is rewarding, rather than have to labour at a job that is very tedious. However, there are many ways to measure job satisfaction. It may be a personal reaction to success or impact in the job, that is to say, achievement rates. Or it may stem from the working atmosphere: working for an inspirational line manager, for example, or with colleagues who are worthy of respect.

In the final analysis, individual circumstances will influence a person's ability to find the job that is right for them, and will also dictate whether they try to keep it in the long term.

READING MODULE

Each question correctly answered scores 1 mark.
CORRECT SPELLING NEEDED IN ALL ANSWERS.

Reading passage 1

Questions 1–13

1 ix 2 x 3 i 4 vii 5 iii 6 viii 7 vi
8 I 9 D 10 B 11 H 12 E 13 A

Reading passage 2

Questions 14–26

14 Y   *Many of those fellow species now seem bound to become extinct*

15 N   *We should at least be thinking in terms of the next million years ... There is nothing in the physical fabric of the Earth or in our own biology to suggest that this is not possible.*

16 Y   *Yet nothing we have so far experienced shows what volcanoes can really do ... Yellowstone could erupt again, and when it does, the whole world will be transformed.*

17 NG   The text talks about asteroids in general and uses the example of an asteroid the size of a small island, but does not say whether Earth is more or less likely to be hit by asteroids of different sizes.

18 N   *If the world does become inhospitable in the next few thousand or million years, then it will probably be our own fault.*

19 NG   The text says that *the difference ... is being made, by politics* and that *Certain kinds of political systems and strategies would predispose us to long-term survival,* but nothing about changes in the way politicians currently in power think.

20 temperature   21 (molten) rock / ash   22 food
23 tidal wave   24 ice age   25 rockets
26 D

Reading passage 3

Questions 27–40

27 I   28 D   29 I   30 E   31 B
32 E   33 C   34 I   35 F
36 metal   37 cardboard   38 wire   39 current
40 water

Notes

Acknowledgements

The authors would like to thank Catriona Watson-Brown for her diligence, good-humoured support and helpful suggestions.

The authors and publishers would like to thank the teachers and consultants who commented on the material:

Singapore: Rosanna Maiolo; Taiwan: Daniel Sansoni; United Arab Emirates: Belinda Hayes; UK: Jan Farndale, Mike Gutteridge; Clare West.

The authors and publishers are grateful to the following for permission to reproduce copyright material. It has not always been possible to identify the sources of all the material used or to contact the copyright holders and in such cases the publishers would welcome information **from the copyright owners.**

Apologies are expressed for any omissions.

p. 4: Open University Press/McGraw-Hill Publishing Company for the adapted text from *Writing at University 2nd Edition* by Crème and Lea. © 2003. Reproduced by kind permission of the Open University Press/McGraw-Hill Publishing Company; p. 6: Scientific American, Inc for adapted text 'Gene Doping' by H Lee Sweeney, © July 2004 by Scientific American, Inc. All rights reserved; p. 8: Tutor2U Limited for adapted text 'Re-branding Skoda', taken from the website www.tutor2u.net. Used by kind permission; p. 11: Oxford University Press, Inc and Hamish Hamilton Ltd for the adapted text from *The State of Language*, by Philip Howard. © 1984 by Hamish Hamilton Ltd. Used by permission of Hamish Hamilton Ltd and Oxford University Press, Inc; p. 12: *New Scientist* for adapted article 'Wrappers smarten up to protect food' by Kurt Kleiner, 24 April 2004, p. 28: adapted article 'Too close for comfort' by David Chandler, 25 June 2005, pp. 48–49: Graphics from 'Gas guzzling planet' 3 September 2005. © New Scientist; p. 14: Rude Girl Publishing for adapted text 'The Internet Debacle', © Janis Ian 2002. All rights reserved. Used by permission; p. 16: The Orion Publishing Group for adapted text from *How Babies Think* by Alison Gopnik, Andrew N Meltzoff and Patricia K Kuhn. Used by permission of Weidenfeld & Nicholson, an imprint of the Orion Publishing Group; p. 19: AMA Research Ltd for the adapted material taken from The Kitchen Appliance Market – UK 2003 Report by AMA Research Ltd, www.amaresearch.co.uk. Used by kind permission; p. 20: Urbanicity Ltd for adapted text 'The World learns from Bogatá', taken from the website www.urbanicity.com. © Urbanicity Ltd; p. 22: Ann Faraday for the adapted text from *The Selling of the Senoi*. Reprinted with permission of Ann Faraday; p. 26 *National Geographic* for adapted text 'Reclaiming the Ancient Manuscripts of Timbuktu' by Chris Ranier, 27 May 2003. Used by permission of Chris Ranier and The National Geographic Image Collection; p. 30: The Australia Institute for adapted text 'Social Implications of Downshifting', taken from the website www.downshifting.net.au. © The Australia Institute; p. 32: Adapted text 'Exploring illness across time and space' taken from the website www.sas.upenn.edu/~rogert.about.html. Used by kind permission of Roger Turner and Christopher Jones; p. 34: The Random House Group for the extract from *The Human Mind* by Robert Winston, published by Bantam Press. Reprinted by permission of the Random House Group Ltd; p. 35: Colin Tudge for the adapted text 'Conscious Objector', *The Guardian* 30 January 2003. Used by permission of Colin Tudge; p. 40: SEEK Ltd for adapted text 'Finding a work/life balance' by Jacqui Tomlins, www.seek.co.nz. Used by permission of SEEK Ltd; p. 42: A & C Black Publishers Ltd for adapted text from *Fashion in Costume* 1200–1980 by Joan Nunn. Used by permission of A & C Black Publishers Ltd; p. 56: FIFA for the adapted text 'More than 2000 years of football' taken from the website http://www.fifa.com. Used by kind permission of FIFA; p. 58 Colin Tudge for adapted text from *So Shall We Reap: What's gone wrong with the world's food – and how to fix it.* (Penguin Books 2004). Copyright Colin Tudge 2004.

The publishers would like to thank the following people for permission to reproduce copyright photographs:

Alamy /© Jeff Morgan p. 9 (t), /© Andre Jenny p. 9 (b), /© D.Hurst p. 16; © AP Photo/Ariana Cubillos p. 20, /© Ben Curtis p. 26 (t); CORBIS/© Tom Stewart p. 4, /© Neil Rabinowitz p. 22, /© Sandro Vannini p. 26 (b); Getty Images/AFP/JACK GUEZ p. 7, /AFP/MARIO VAZQUEZ p. 36, /Bongarts/Vladimir Rys p. 40, /The Image Bank/Siqui Sanchez p. 32 (b), /Koichi Kamoshida p. 34, /Graeme Robertson p. 42, /John Stanton p. 14, /Stone/UHB Trust p. 35 (r), /Taxi/Willie Maldonado p. 30; Photolibrary.com/Picture Press/Wartenberg p. 6; © Science Photo Library p. 35 (l), /TEK IMAGE p. 32 (t); © SKODA p. 8; www.temptimecorp.com p. 12; © Elizabeth Whiting and Associates p. 19.

Key: l = left, r = right, c = centre, t = top, b = bottom

The publishers are grateful to the following illustrators:

Gillian Martin: pp. 5, 10, 21, 38, 41, 47;
Kamae Design: pp. 24, 28, 48, 49.

The publishers are grateful to the following contributors:

Catriona Watson-Brown: editorial work
Hilary Fletcher: photographic direction, picture research